THE *Flamingo* ADVANTAGE

HOW TO LEVERAGE UNIQUE, STAY RELEVANT AND CHANGE THE WORLD

- KATIE HORNOR -

AUTHOR OF FAITH LIKE FLAMINGOS

The Flamingo Advantage

How to Leverage Unique, Stay Relevant and Change the World

by Katie Hornor

Hardback ISBN-13: 978-1-7346046-5-8

Paperback ISBN-13: 978-1-7346046-4-1

Digital ISBN-13: 978-1-7346046-6-5

Pre-released as "Flamingo Marketing" 2022. Original cover and interior design © 2022 by Katie Hornor. Cover & interior photos by Canva. Interior comic art by Kirsi Belle Hornor of www.HumorUs.co. All art used by permission. All rights reserved. Edited by Dawnita Fogleman of www.PrairieDustTrail.com.

Unless otherwise noted all Scripture quotations are from the *Holy Bible*, King James Version (KJV).

Printed in the USA.

Dedication:

To My Husband, Tap:

Thank you for sharing the vision, the adventure
and the rewards with me. I love you always.

To You, Dear Reader:

No matter what "they" say, you *are* unique.
Your message *does* matter.
And I pray that the message of this book will empower you to
See the new things God is bringing into existence for you.
That it will help you to see
Your God as the Benevolent Owner of the Business,
Your Work as your Sacred Duty,
Your People as Eternal Souls, and
Your Business Activities as an Act of Worship
that can create a Legacy of Impact...
So that you may experience the Fulfillment and Joy
of being part of His larger Kingdom Plan.

Table of Contents

Praise for Katie Hornor and

The Flamingo Advantage

"In I Corinthians 3, The Apostle Paul expresses concern about having the ability to speak freely from the Lord if he was being paid by those people hearing his preaching. Thus, to maintain that freedom, he chose to continue providing for his personal needs by doing "secular" work he was gifted in doing. Surely he was "called" to ministry yet he did not abdicate his abilities to support himself. Like Paul, we can choose to see our work as our best vehicle for ministry. We fulfill our calling by using the work gifts God has given us. Katie has given us the guide to change the world - as we are blessed to be a blessing."

Dan Miller
Author of *48 Days to the Work You Love*
48Days.com

"Katie Hornor is one of the most helpful and encouraging individuals I know. Her technique is quality, her demeanor is professional and her coaching is both Bible-based and achievable. Our family income has continued to grow as a result of working with her. If you are a Christian in business, I highly recommend that you read this book."

Dawnita Fogleman
Author of *Star Chronicles: A Bible Based Study of the Stars*
PrairieDustTrail.com

"Katie is a wonderful coach; rooted in Christ and savvy in business. Her courses and coaching have hugely benefitted me over the last few years and I am so excited to see her foundational materials coming out in this book!"

Danielle Tate
Author of *Restoring The Lost Petal: Recovering from the Loss of Sexual Purity*
DanielleTate.org

"Katie Hornor's practical application of God's Word is life changing. She follows God's Word in her business, her teaching and her writing and *The Flamingo Advantage* is no exception. Get ready for a boost of confidence in your business and your life."

Myrna Stiles Buckles
Founder of Legacy in Action

"Katie taught me the difference between doing business for God and doing business *with* God and I'm thrilled to see this powerful content coming out now in *The Flamingo Advantage*. Read it, you won't be disappointed."

Kathy Burrus
Author of *EnVision YOU: Unstuck and Confident*
KathyBurrus.com

"*The Flamingo Advantage* will change your life. This message is ground breaking. We've been taught to keep business in a separate pocket from spiritual life, and yet the truth is God wants to use all of us every moment. I have been through this content with Katie 7 times (side note: so glad she's finally putting it into book form). Initially I gained calmness and confidence to move forward, and every time since God has grown me, grown my business, and more importantly grown my opportunities to impact people for Him. I cannot recommend it enough."

Brenda Parmelee
Author of *The 31-Day Guide to Create Your Clutter Free Home Oasis*
SmallerLivingHugeLife.com

"The revelation of what God's definition of success is as it relates to business and marketing and how it's so much different than what I thought it was changed my business. I appreciate so much the Scripture that Katie pulls from in her teaching to inform our beliefs from God's Word rather than solely contemporary best practices."

Nancy Todd
OilsFirstBlog.com

In her book *The Flamingo Advantage*, Katie Hornor gives faith-based entrepreneurs the clarity and confidence they need to operate in their God-given marketplace assignment!"

Matt Tommey
Artist, Author & Mentor at MattTommeyMentoring.com

"We are often told that business and faith don't mix; that to be successful at one, you need to sacrifice the other. However, Katie Hornor shows you that the two were always meant to be one. Katie's teachings changed my life and my business. She has taught me that Christians can be successful and honor God with their success. I can preach the Gospel through my programs and services without being a preacher. I can have a ministry through my business even if the business in not a non-profit. I can have an impact that's not valued by income. The skills I gained through her fabulous programs have allowed me to move to my dream home in another state and have given me confidence, vision, and success. I am building a legacy and this is where it started."

Jennifer Anne Elia
ScaleMyBusinessOnLinkedIn.com

"I thought God needed to help me with my business but Katie showed me that God is the owner of my business, I work for Him and serve Him by serving those He brings to me. Katie's principles are always based in God's Word and she reminds us to always go back to that truth as we seek to share His Kingdom. In *The Flamingo Advantage*, Katie shares the truth that "business is about what God wants to do for others through the abilities He's entrusted to you." He has given me a great responsibility to care for and love His people with the gifts He has given me. The teaching from this book has changed my whole perspective on business and life. It is not about me, it is about God and as long as I keep that truth at the center of my business, He will bring me all I need to be successful. I am so grateful to Katie for her wisdom and guidance and always bringing me back to God's truth!"

Tresa Rolando Salters
Livewellblessed.com

"One often thinks of marketing as advertising, selling and convincing a buyer. The way Katie talks about marketing in *F The Flamingo Advantage* is that instead of advertising, one is sharing. Instead of selling, one is serving. Instead of convincing, one is teaching. Instead of being slick, one behaves like Christ. When you follow His principles, you know you are doing the right thing and on the correct path. You can have fun while working and fulfilling the purpose He has had for you all along."

PJ Pitonyak
Grief to Life Coach & ESL Teacher at WonderandGraceLifeCoaching.com"

"After 44 years as a CPA in small business and taxes, I have lived through several economic seasons as a Christian business person. I believe there's no more important time than now to be all that Christ needs us to be in our own marketplaces. Everyone is riding the waves of our current economic storm looking for those that are grounded to something stronger to lead them. As we co-create our businesses with the Lord He uses us to be that grounding. For those of us seeking grounding and strength, *The Flamingo Advantage* is a must read! Katie has shown me the importance of seeing myself as God sees me in order for me to carry out His unique plan in my business world. *The Flamingo Advantage* helps you understand how to stand strong in biblical truths, lean into your unique gifting, and go forth into a world that most definitely needs you to shine Christ's light in all you do. As you read this book please allow yourself to be open to all new ideas, to allow God's Spirit to speak to you in a unique way and help you understand more fully the flamingo He intends you to be in your life and your business. Remember He loves you too much to leave you where you are."

Connie Buskohl
CPA, Sioux Falls, SD

"As a pastor's wife and missionary on the field, I had the typical ministry mindset that made it hard for me not to give everything away. I was looking for biblical backing to help me be comfortable with earning money and I found it in what Katie teaches here."

Terrie Yandall

"*The Flamingo Advantage* offers fun, unconventional strategies, secrets, and tactics for earning your relevance to change the world and earn big profits from your adventures while doing so!"

David L. Hancock
Author of *Performance-Driven Giving: The Roadmap To Unleashing The Power Of Generosity In Your Life*

"I had forgotten God's grace and provision and felt like I was a failure. But after studying with Katie in the course that became the book *The Flamingo Advantage*, I learned to transfer ownership of my business to God and step into my role as CEO, and that's when I learned to see his goodness and I found freedom to grow our family business. I expect you will too as you read."

Hope Ware
UnderTheMedian.com

"Remember how passionate and energized you were when you started your business? *The Flamingo Advantage* will reignite your passion for the work God has called you to do. Katie's enthusiasm for finding God's best in your business is colorful and contagious!"

Ryan Steuer
CEO of MagnifyLearningIN.org

"Katie teaches a philosophy of business we are not hearing about in today's business culture. She teaches how to understand your faith position in business. To understand who you are and who your God is within the confines of that business by navigating through Scripture...It is a counter-cultural business philosophy that will outlive the latest fads and help you secure a good foundation for the sacred duty to which you have been called."

Kris Fasse
Integrative Health Coach

"What excuses are blocking you from pursuing those deeply buried dreams? Katie lovingly and boldly calls you out in *The Flamingo Advantage* Warning! As you journey through her story every myth you're believing will be exposed to God's truth and breath new life into your story. Ready to Flamingo?"

Mark Ross
Artist, Thought Partner, Encorepreuer at Next Thing Group

"*The Flamingo Advantage* is absolutely amazing. There are so many pithy truths in this Christian business manual, not the least of which is the Scripture quoted throughout. Perhaps my favorite quote from Katie is "He's going to put those desires in your heart, which are things He wants to fulfill. It's almost as if He's saying, "I'm going to place in her a desire for this, because I want to see her delight when she receives (or achieves) it. Business is about what God wants to do for others through the abilities He's entrusted to you."

Sandra Angelo
Faith Based Creative Life Coach at SandraAngelo.com

"*The Flamingo Advantage* truly spoke to my spirit. Learning that God is my business owner ("The Owner"), who has entrusted me as the CEO has been so freeing. As entrepreneurs we can feel the pressure to perform and deliver so keenly. Knowing that God is ultimately responsible for the success of my business, while my part is to partner, steward, and cultivate the resources along with the unique skills and abilities I've been gifted, has provided me with such a sense of assurance. Katie provides practical, Biblically based steps, both simple and powerful, to help you make decisions and take action with your business with God's will in mind. No more endless second guessing or fretting as I now understand I just need to be faithful, show up each day and live in my calling. Katie showed how I can show up as my authentic self, and bring Christ into the marketplace through love for my clients. I can show up proud of the services I provide to them with confidence and power exactly the way I was intended to do it - with my own unique flamingo advantage!"

Kristin Engen
KristinEngen.com

"I love the creative way Katie lays out this book. She reminds us of the unique skill set God has bestowed upon us to do what He has created us to do. She shuts down the myths so many Christians have heard with Biblical Truth. If you want success in your business God's way, this book needs to be in your tool kit!"

Caris Snider
Author of *Anxiety Elephants*
CarisSnider.com

"*The Flamingo Advantage* is a great book if you want to learn more about how to incorporate faith into your business and your life for the world to see! In life, we ask for God's guidance, in business we sometimes forget to ask for it. We get stuck in the mode of sales and marketing, do this, do that, make money.... We forget to incorporate God into businesses success. God has His hand in everything, it's our job to follow His lead and do things as He would want. So many points in this book ring true: how God sees us in our lives, how to be successful, and how money and building our businesses is a part of that success. Katie sees that giving information isn't enough, she also gives us the space to *own* the information."

Christine Odle
Author of *Rockin' Your Business Finances*
ChristineOdle.com

"This book will help Christian business owners bridge the gap between their spiritual life and business life. It's a must-read for any Christian who needs a fresh infusion of inspiration to remind you of your greater WHY. It's a powerful reminder to invite God into every area of your business so that you can experience joy, purpose, and impact on the path He has for you. *The Flamingo Advantage* is a call to step up and play a bigger game—to take the leap of faith into your big dreams as the highest expression of your faith in God to see them through—for His purposes. Thank you Katie for such an inspiring, powerful book!"

Michelle Lange
Video Marketing & Online Launch Expert, Founder, Visible Impact

"As someone who loves processes and helping others discover the uniqueness in who God created them to be, I love how Katie has captured both the being and the doing in this wonderful book. Guiding us through finding our own unique self and all while also uncovering all the myths that hold us back from living into the work God has for us to bring about and leave our legacy. *The Flamingo Advantage* is a go-to resource for spreading the gospel as an entrepreneur!"

Teresa McCloy
Creator & Founder, REALIFE Process® Coach
Author of *Do What Matters: Live from Rest not Rush*

"*The Flamingo Advantage* takes you through actionable steps to align your business with your faith and make both stronger. The page-turning lessons and insights create a solid platform for you to build off of as you are growing your business. Katie has broken down the complex into bite-sized actionable steps. If you want to create a business aligned with your faith, *The Flamingo Advantage* is a highly-recommended must read."

Tina Brandau
SPRH, SHRM-SCP
Author of *Standing Strong: The Real Life Story of Overcoming Adversity and Becoming Unstoppable in Life and Business*

Find More of Katie's Books at

www.theflamingoadvantage.com/books/

Acknowledgments

When I think of who I should be grateful for in this whole writing/publishing journey, I have to begin with my **God**. My always good, ever-faithful, ever-present, all-knowing, all-powerful, all-loving, showing favor though I don't deserve it, heavenly Father and King. He has graciously walked with me every step of this journey and I want to publicly acknowledge here all that He continues to do both privately and publicly. No experience or opportunity is wasted with Him, and I couldn't ask for, dream of or even imagine a better boss.

Secondly, I want to thank my amazing husband, best friend and business partner, **Tap**. I love you always and forever. Thank you for the example you are, the strength you give, for loving me back in spite of my quirks and being my biggest fan.

To our children: I don't know what I'd do without any of you. You're truly my favorite people in the world!

To my daughter, **Butterfly:** you made me mom and I know no one else who loves all things beautiful as you do. Thank you for inspiring me to embrace the mess, live in awe and continually be open to new people and experiences.

To my daughter, **Belle:** thank you for sharing your talents of humor and art with our readers in this book. I am constantly amazed at your wit, talent and gift of reading people. Thank you for being my office buddy throughout this writing process and for keeping the mood light when the days got long.

To my first born son, **Sir:** thank you for teaching me to find joy in numbers without being defined by them. Thank you for your heart to serve and your ability to make even accounting enjoyable.

To my son, (who asked to be called here) **The Muffin Man**... your courage inspires me every day. Your story is so tied to the flamingo trip that started this whole adventure. I want you to know how grateful I am to get to be your mom.

To my daughter, **Sunshine**: Your hugs make every day better. Your smiles, songs and laughter are such a blessing to me. I love that you can make up songs like your great Grandpa, and I can't wait to see what God does with your flamingo advantage as you grow.

To my Dad and Mom: you were the first people I ever met who saw business as an avenue of ministry. Thank you for your ongoing example of using business assets, relationships and opportunities to be the hands and feet of Jesus in the world.

To My Queens Mastermind Members - as of this publishing: Brenda, Cherie, Connie, Dawnita, Danielle, Emmie, Jennifer, Kathy, Myrna, Nancy, PJ, Tresa, Rachel... Thank you for your loyalty to the unique work God's called you to do. Your labor is not in vain in the Lord, and your care for one another challenges me to greater love.

Dawnita Fogleman - Thank you for your mad editing skills and gracious corrections when I muddled up Spanish and English grammar. Thank you for your loyal friendship through the years.

Ellie Shefi - Thank you for sharing from your publishing knowledge to make the book even better.

Nancy Leigh DeMoss Woglemuth - Thank you for inspiring me as a young girl to transcribe these important lessons for legacy impact.

Jim Berg - I read the pre-release copy of your book *Changed Into His Image* as a 16 year old and was forever changed. Your teaching was foundational to God's work in my life over the next few critical years of preparation for ministry and I am forever grateful.

Andy Andrews - My gratitude is expressed best in your own words: "There are generations yet unborn, whose very lives will be shifted and shaped by the moves you make and the actions you take... tonight. And tomorrow. And tomorrow night. And the next day. And the next." Thank you for writing *The Noticer* and shifting mine.

Mardi Collier - Thank you for writing and publishing your book *What Do I Know About My God?*. Thank you for the encouragement to always and always and always go back to the truth of who God is. This has changed my life and my business forever.

Jana Lynn Gephart - Thank you for introducing me to musicals and extreme party planning. In spite of the vast differences in our worlds, you've now been my best friend for 68% of my life - and counting. I praise God for the day He created you so beautifully unique, I celebrate the day we met, and thank God for a friendship that never stops loving. You're the best!

Joon Han - Thank you for making the obvious obvious to me and for helping me see my own flamingo advantage. Thank you for showing me I didn't need permission when I had a right.

Angus Nelson - Thank you for pushing me to embrace my flamingo-ness with boldness, and teaching Tap and I to dream together.

Bari Baumgardner - I couldn't ask for a better example of a coach who cares so deeply about excellence and her clients' success. Thank you for encouraging me to embrace "The Flamingo Advantage" as a title as well as a formula, framework and movement. I knew you were amazing the first time I saw you in action. I am still amazed that the dream of working with you came true. If I can serve with half the love you do, I know we'll change the world.

Jeff Walker - I will be eternally grateful for your annual river trip that led you to a hike through the canyon to see a handprint on the wall that became a story you would share at an event and forever change the trajectory of my life and my business. Thank you for creating a business that sees people as people, not income, and a caring community that welcomed me in, gave me a home when no one else would, and challenged me to dream bigger than I ever dared to dream before. I want to be like you when I grow up.

Dan Miller - I longed for a champion for more than a decade. Thank you for standing in the gap and welcoming me to your *Eaglepreneur* community with open arms.

Dean Graziosi - Your family first commitment and consistency inspire me every day. Thank you for the work you do and the love with which you do it.

Barry Friedman - Thank you for being the coach who asks the tough questions and for believing in Tap and I when we couldn't believe for ourselves. You somehow always know the right thing to ask or say.

Rachel Pedersen - Thank you for inspiring me with your example of flamingo-ness. I so appreciate and gain courage from watching you be you in life and business.

Des O'Neill - Thank you for seeing me, for speaking life and encouragement to a drowning soul in a sea full of people who didn't notice. The world needs more people like you.

Cathy Hay - You'll always be Queen in my book. I'll never forget your example of embracing your God-gifted uniqueness regardless of popular opinion or critique. I strive to exude the kindness and care that comes so easily from you.

Though it may sound strange, I also want to express gratefulness to the many souls and organizations whose policies, actions and examples have instructed me as to how I don't want to treat people and run a business.

I respect that we each get to choose how to manage the business we've been entrusted with and though not always easy or pleasant experiences, I am grateful for the perspective and wisdom I've gained from our interactions.

And finally, to **Aaron Walker, Darren Shearer**, **Matt Tommey**, **Ray Edwards** and my dear friend **Connie Buskohl, CPA:** Thank you for exemplifying what a Christian in the marketplace looks like. You have been a breath of fresh air and a sweet savour of the presence of God to me. I have utmost respect for each of you.

About the Author

Katie Hornor is a prolific Christian author, business strategy coach for coaches and course businesses and an international keynote speaker.

Katie and her husband, Tap, left all they had in the United States for a ministry opportunity overseas, only to have their dreams pulled out from under them. The Hornors bounced back to build a business in their second language among the fastest growing market demographic in the world, and then began teaching what they had learned to coach English Speakers.

Katie has +created 25 online courses and self-published over 50 books including *Faith Like Flamingos: The Christian Business Guide to Walking Out Your Faith in Bold Color* and 9 other best-sellers.

Her Christian Business Podcast, *The Flamingo Advantage,* provides inspiring interviews and practical marketing and business training from a biblical perspective and airs several times per week on all the main podcast platforms as well as YouTube.

Katie's inspirational story of ex-missionary to six-figure expat business owner began over 12 years ago at her kitchen table while balancing a baby on her lap. In 2022, she was named one of the top 10 entrepreneurs to watch by FOX, NBC and CBS. Katie's Master's degree in Education and teaching experience in different fields has distinguished her as a leader in the world of online courses and curriculum development.

Having studied under some of the biggest names in the speaker, influencer & online marketing space, Katie has been welcomed on their stages and has quickly become the go-to resource for her "experience first" and "business as worship" methods and mindset.

The key to her success begins with submitting all to the knowledge and leading of God as the Owner of her business, while implementing systems for mastery, then iterating and always including an element of fun and a view towards legacy impact.

Katie's Bible-based marketing and student experience strategies have helped clients double their income, let their spouses retire, and create businesses they enjoy - all without compromising their faith, their family or their values.

Born in Binghamton, NY, in 1979, Katie currently serves her people from her home abroad in Campeche, México where she and her husband manage their online businesses, local airbnb[1], and continued speaking ministry. The Hornors do all this while continuing the non-traditional education of their five children, three of whom currently have roles in the family business.

Invite Katie to speak at your next event by visiting www.KatieHornor.com

Katie's Podcast: TheFlamingoAdvantage.com/podcast

Connect with Katie on Social Media:

YouTube: @KatieHornorFlamingoAdvantage
IG: @KatieHornor @christian_business_events
Facebook: www.facebook.com/katie.hornor
LinkedIn: @KatieHornor
T: @Katie_Hornor
P: @KatieHornor

Get in touch to learn about the following programs and events:

- **Christian Marketing Retreat** - live event: How to Effectively Market your Business as a Believer in the Marketplace www.FlamingoBizEvent.com
- **The Flamingo Advantage Framework™**: Bible-based principles and Frameworks for marketing and client experience for modern Christians in business www.TheFlamingoAdvantage.com
- **Flamboyance™ Group Coaching:** Grow Your Business by implementing sound frameworks into a scaleable business process that

won't compromise your faith, family or non-negotiables www.TheFlamingoAdvantage.com

- **The Queens Mastermind™:** Create a Business that Provides the Lifestyle and room for Legacy Activities that Light You Up in our Women's Higher-Level Business Mastermind www.QueensMastermind.com

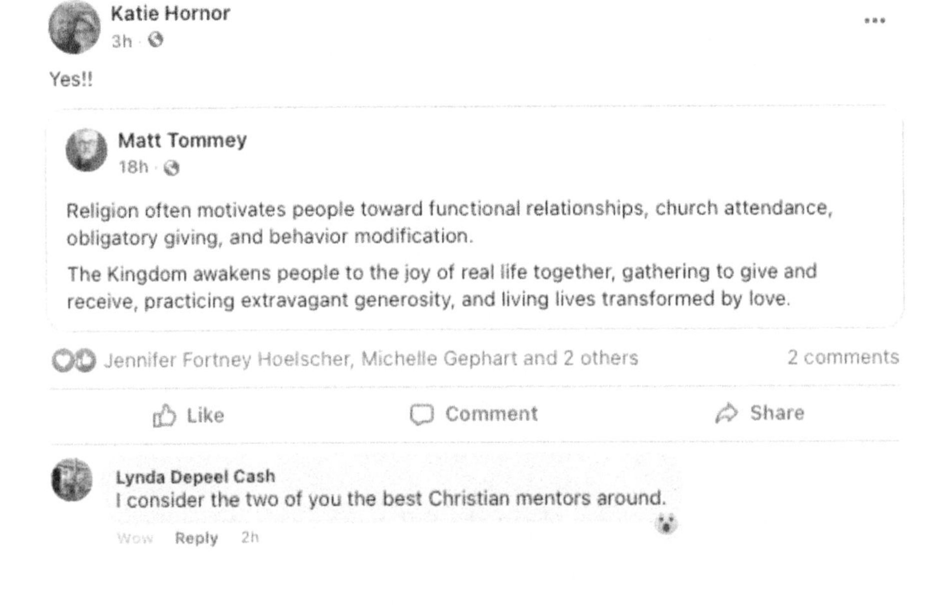

LET'S GET STARTED!
#HUMORUSCO

"NO ONE IN THE WORLD DOES WHAT YOU DO LIKE YOU DO."

KATIE HORNOR

But ask the beasts, and they will teach you;
the birds of the heavens, and they will tell you.
Job 12:7

Flamingos are the world's best example of organic marketers. Their intrinsic uniqueness renders them famous in both the animal and human kingdoms. Their reputation precedes them as one of the most outlandish, out of place looking creatures who are strangely solidly at home in the wild environment in which they have been placed. Criticisms don't phase them. Storms don't ruffle their feathers. They don't even work hard at marketing how amazing they are. They just are and we flock to them.

The ecosystems in which the flamingos exist depend on them being them, depend on them doing what they were created to do for the world to continue to prosper and flourish - a duty they embrace with their whole being, for how could they choose otherwise? Their faithfulness in doing what they were created to do is relevant to the success of the habitats and all of the other beings who interact in their world every single day.

And should there be a shift in their world, a disease that diminishes their numbers, that change initiates ripples across the globe that is felt on nearly every continent. One colony of quirky odd little birds can change the world. As can you.

Scripture tells us you are a unique being. God formed you in your mother's womb. (Jeremiah 1:5) Before you were born He knew you and called you by name. (Isaiah 49:1). He has plans for you that are peaceful and specific. (Jeremiah 29:11) You being your own quirky self has a purpose and an impact in this world, this ecosystem, this unique time in history in which God has placed you on earth. If you embrace that uniqueness, your marketing will become easier and more effective. You only need to be you, creating awareness of the glory of your Creator God to market well who you are and what you do.

You being you and doing what you were created to do with your unique gifting in this world contributes to the success of the whole body of Christ. (Romans 12, Galatians 5-6) Others depend upon you doing your part so that they can flourish in theirs every single day and faithfulness begets success (Proverbs 28:20, Matthew 25:23).

Your choice to fully embrace being authentically you in the marketplace, your choice to glorify God by doing what He created you to do in the place He created you to do it has an impact which ripples across the globe and can be felt on every continent. When you, my friend, learn to see your unique abilities and position in Christ as a pink advantage, as an opportunity to be leveraged to maintain a relevant presence in a world that needs Christ, and impact your marketplace ecosystem, God can change the world through you!

PART ONE

Leverage UNIQUE

THE WORLD NEEDS MORE BELIEVERS IN BUSINESS UNAFRAID TO EMBRACE THEIR FLAMINGO ADVANTAGE

1. Facing Reality: THERE IS NO NEW NORMAL

There is no new thing under the sun.

Ecclesiastes 1:9

My daughter and I were packing up our display table at a Christian women's conference and trade show in Monterrey, Mexico the day the world went crazy. The anxiety was palpable as we began to hear of attendees who couldn't get home because their flights had been canceled and their countries' borders closed. Thankfully, we did make it home and almost didn't get to leave again for two long years.

Just as those in my grandparent's generation remember where they were when they heard the news of Pearl Harbor, my parent's generation remember getting their first personal computer in the early 1980s, and my generation remembers where we were when we heard the news of the 9/11 attacks on the World Trade Center... so our children's generation will always remember where they were when the world shut down for a global pandemic in 2020.

The world, as we know it, is changing. As much as we wish it were otherwise, when events such as these touch us so deeply and intimately as a culture and as individuals, things are never again the same.

And yet, in an uncertain world it is possible to have unshakable clarity as to what God wants for you and your business. It is possible to know the formula for consistent peace and to have a system that allows you to make confident decisions. Even during times like these, you can grow your business grounded in your faith and God's plan for you.

As a woman of faith, a wife, a mom, a business coach and entrepreneur with over 20 years of ministry and business experience, I've been teaching Christians with course businesses and coaching programs how to overcome their fears and grow their businesses through the power of God's truth since 2014.

Every challenge you face is an invitation to know God better.

I believe every challenge you face is a pivot point. Each one an invitation to know God better, to embrace His promises for your future, and to step into His plan to use you in the Kingdom.

Having taught the material presented in this book to thousands of believers in business, I can estimate that 99% of the Christian entrepreneurs I've met want confidence, peace of mind and results in their business. And I can say with 100% surety those things are only achieved by doing business with God, not apart from Him.

In the year after the pandemic, it's estimated that more than 160,000 small businesses came to a permanent close due to the various effects and demands of Coronavirus[2]. And yet *Forbes* Business reported that US retail online shopping was expected to go up 68% over the previous year[3].

Then just as quickly it seems, the world started again and the US Census Bureau stats tell us that 4.4 million people filed new business applications in 2021 and that was to be surpassed in 2022 by an estimated 5.4 million new business applications.[4]

The surge of new businesses caused its own market crisis creating more competition in the marketplace, specifically in remote work industries and online spaces. Competition is not a bad thing but this sudden influx has created confusion as consumers now have to be more discerning when choosing between start ups who may look amazing but have little experience and more established businesses who may be in need of a facelift.

Based on all of this, I truly believe there is no better time than right now as a believer in the marketplace, to learn how applying God's principles to your business will give you clarity, confidence, and vision. This, in turn will help you to embrace your flamingo advantage, the unique part you play in His Kingdom plan to grow your business and to grow your impact for Christ in the world.

I'll be backing up all my claims with God's Word. God's Word is powerful and living. Even if you've heard it before, I want you to invite the Lord to open your heart and teach you something new from what you're reading. Don't be one of "those people" who cross their arms and say: *"This doesn't apply to me."*

You bought this book after all. You must have thought there'd be something you could learn from it. Be open to it. God's Word applies to you because you are His child, period. It has nothing to do with the actual niche of your business and everything to do with your position as His child and chosen ambassador. The practical application principles from God's Word apply universally regardless of the type of business He's called you into. So don't get hung up on that. Ask the Holy Spirit to show you how this applies to you and how you can walk this out in your daily business.

The days are short my friend. Your message matters. People need what God has gifted you to offer. So if you're ready to hear from God about how to market and grow your business, join me in the following chapters.

Note: At the end of each chapter you'll see our "time for reflection" comic and a few prompts to help you document what stands out to you as you read. Don't be afraid to write in the book. Think of it as a textbook, a journal, a coloring book...whatever you need to be able to capture and remember what God shows you here.

TIME FOR *Reflection*

Now unto him that is able to do exceeding abundantly above all that we ask or think, according to the power that worketh in us, unto him be glory in the church by Christ Jesus throughout all ages, world without end.

Ephesians 3:20-21

Seven months pregnant, and toting a toddler, my husband Tap and I crossed the southern Arizona border into Mexico on Friday the 13th of April, 2007, to finally realize our dream of being missionaries. We had just finished a two year tour traveling around the US inviting individuals and churches to give donations and pledge financial support so God could minister through us at a Bible college in Mexico.

Two years later the Lord moved our little family from there to Campeche, Mexico, on the bottom coast of the Gulf of Mexico, near the Cancun Peninsula to minister at a children's home.

It was a hard move. We didn't just change ministries, we changed mission boards, which is a notoriously sticky situation, and we sustained a lot of damage in the process.

The ministry that we left wasn't happy that we left, to put it mildly. The defamation and betrayal by those we'd considered friends wounded us deeply. We ended up losing emotional support and a lot of financial support... but we knew God was calling us to the children's home.

Our new purpose was to grow into the leadership role of this work as the widowed missionary woman retired and shepherd the ministry into the future, whatever God had. We imagined we'd be there forever. We imagined our grown children someday bringing their children back to visit...

All of those sweet imaginations dissipated quickly when nine months after our arrival she explained that her national staff had not been on board with her decision to bring us in as leadership. They had not changed their minds as she'd hoped and we would have to leave.

Just like that, in a matter of less than 12 months, we'd had two unsavory ministry changes. More people lost faith in us. More ministry donors stopped supporting us.

At the same time, there was an economic crisis in the States. As the economy crashed it became convenient for churches to say, "Oh, well, you know, you failed. We're not supporting you anymore." It eventually reached the point that we didn't know from one month to the next how much money we'd have to live on for the next month. At one very pivotal moment in our story, now with four small children to care for, we had five dollars left in the bank, no savings, no credit cards, no work visa here and literally no way to get back to the States, even if we'd wanted to. All we could do was ask the Lord: "What do you want us to do?"

We had been living and working for so long under a palpable fear of man, asking with every decision we made "Will "they" agree with this? Who's going to stop supporting us if we do X, Y, or Z, and they don't approve?" that we really didn't know what it meant to follow God's leading.

Over the next few months and years, as God led us to start our own business, overcoming incredible obstacles and criticisms, the Lord began to tenderly teach us who He is, what that meant for us, for our children, for our ministry, for our business, and for the people we served and would come to serve in the future.

Everything I'm sharing with you in this book has come through the fire. God has walked Tap and I through it. We have lived it. We teach it to our children and to our clients and students.

In 2011, God led us to start a company that was the first, and for a decade the only, literature-based homeschool curriculum company that existed in the Spanish language providing curriculum and materials to homeschool families with children aged preschool through sixth grade.

Then, the Lord allowed us to host the very first in history that we know of, online annual homeschool summit for Spanish-speaking families.

Next we added a membership community for Spanish-speaking homeschool moms that's since been entrusted to one of our long-time assistants in the business to run as its own stand alone business under her guidance and care.[5]

We thought we'd be a little 30 person ministry in the middle of nowhere in Mexico that nobody had ever heard of - forever. And the Lord just continued to grow things until we had a ministry that reached around the world. We started training Christian business owners in 2014 to grow their online course businesses and coaching programs for greater legacy impact.

Prior to getting started we had plenty of professional education but very little business background. We had to learn how to create a website. We had to learn what HTML was. We had to learn how to do marketing. We had to learn to do financial accounting. We had to figure out how to create products and offers and how to make our own graphics and do social media.

Every single thing we had to learn, one step at a time, and the Lord was faithful through it all, allowing us to take what we'd learned, like in 2 Timothy 2:2, and teach it to faithful people who would be able to teach it to others as well.

At some point, I was able to synthesize what the Lord had been teaching us in terms of how to do business from a biblical perspective, from a God first perspective. That became a course called *Doing Business with God*™. We've now taught that course nearly a dozen times to over 300 people in a small group settings. It has become the basis for everything we teach from our free masterclasses to our high ticket coaching and mastermind programs.

You *must* know who God is, because that is the basis of everything that you believe and those beliefs influence every thing that you think and say and do in life and in business.

Doing Business with God[6] teaches how to make decisions with confidence and with clarity and purpose so that you can be the best at what God has called you to do. Our students learn how to evaluate what they do in business, and how God is leading them, according to His Word.

All of us are called, practically, to serve the Lord in different areas. But the thing that we have in common is that we've all been called to bring Him glory through the varied gifts and talents that He has given us.

And... every business needs a bit of pruning now and then. So in 2018, we "broke" our good business and began reimagining it. We asked ourselves and the Lord: *"What would our business look like if we could do more of the things that bring us joy, make a bigger impact in the world and give us a life we don't feel the need to vacation from?"*

In 2019, after a family trip to see flamingos in the wild, I began writing a book called *Faith Like Flamingos: The Christian Business Guide to Walking Out Your Faith in Bold Color*[7], not knowing that the Christian business analogies from those quirky pink birds would become a bestseller that would open doors in ballrooms and zoom rooms and social media settings all over the world for God to do His work through me.

Yet that is exactly what God did, and during the biggest global pandemic of a century, the Lord saw fit to 5x our business revenues, grow our team, strengthen our marriage and family and give us the desires of our heart.

And then He said: *"Write the next book. More people need to know that my favor and power is not limited. That they do not need to be afraid to honor me with what I've created them to do. More need to experience the freedom that comes from marketing and doing business with me."*

So, that's what got us here, to this book, and to you.

I need you to know that my family, my team and I have prayed for you. Prayed that you would find this book right when you need it. Prayed that your eyes would be opened, your understanding would be opened and your heart would be ready to receive whatever special message the Holy Spirit has for you, and that through this reading experience you also will make the commitment to leverage your God-given uniqueness to stay relevant to the people He's bringing to you to serve so that by the power of His Spirit He can change the world through you!

For Reflection:

My biggest takeaway from this chapter is....

The truth I need to act on is...

My action will be...

I will take this action on/by (date)...

3. Abdicated TO DIVINE OWNERSHIP

Now therefore, if ye will obey my voice indeed, and keep my covenant, then ye shall be a peculiar treasure unto me above all people: for all the earth is mine:

Exodus 19:5

You've heard of DOB right? Date of birth. And DBA? Doing business as... but have you heard of DBO: Divine Business Ownership? When I was a teenager I read a book by Stanley Tam entitled *God Owns My Business*[8]. I remember that it struck a chord deep within me that would vibrate quietly there for the next 25 years.

It was quite popular when I was growing up that Christians would claim one should "make God your copilot." There were shirts and keychains and other merchandise bearing the slogan. I remember feeling in my heart that this was a bit theologically off kilter. I mean, I was old enough to understand that God says in His Word He is sovereign. He is already in the future and knows what will happen. I was old enough to read that

He is all wise and all knowing ... So why in the world would I be wanting Him to be the copilot?! He should be the pilot, shouldn't He? Shouldn't the one who is the most qualified be flying the plane, driving the car, running the show?

Looking back on it now, I am grateful that the Holy Spirit was cautioning me even then against culture's mis-alignment of God's Truth with regards to who "runs the show" in one's life and business.

One of the big themes we see in Scripture having to do with life and business is the theme of the farmer. My dad grew up on a dairy farm in upstate New York, and though he's long been out of that industry, he still raises a few organic cows on his land each year. In fact, as I write this he's just sent me a photo of the new calf named Liberty, who took some liberties at one day old and crossed the fences getting lost in the woods and having to be rescued... so, a lot of the stories I have about farming come secondhand, but it's not as distant as some people who've only ever driven by a farm...

The sowing and reaping illustrations found in Scripture show God as the Creator and Sovereign. They portray Him as the One who is in control of all things. God created natural laws that work whether or not you believe in Him. They work much better when you do things *with* Him. But even if you deny Him, they will work.

The farmer knows that if he plants corn, corn will grow. That's the natural law. The spiritual law gives the farmer the promise of wisdom when he asks of God (James 1:5). God will direct him to authoritative resources to tell him when to plant, what kind of soil preparation is optimal, how much and how often to water, what type of fertilization is best, and when is the best moment to harvest...

The lesson is that God provides. That is His nature. And the more you know Him as your provider, the more success you can have in what He's called you to do.

What we sow into our businesses, God will bless simply because of His character and the natural laws He's put in place. When we sow into our business, in alignment with His Word and the wisdom and leading of the Holy Spirit, we can reap much more bountiful rewards.

The reality is, there are natural results that happen when you do certain things. If you look at it as God's seed, God's money or God's time that you're stewarding and investing into this, for the good of God's business, then you can open up an entirely new world of greater opportunities, results and impact. This is what you're doing when you run the business *with* God. When you put Him in the position of "owner" of the business. When you are conscious of who God is as your provider; when in everything you do you come back to the question *"Who is my God?"* and based on the truth of who He is you then ask, *"What is my next right step?"* Your beliefs affect your thoughts, which affect your actions and your words. If you are believing wrongly about who God is in relation to your business, you will think wrongly. And when you're thinking wrongly, your words and actions can be wrong, and then things get all mismatched and mixed up and don't come out the way you intended.

In farming, there's an expectation that when you plant a seed in the ground, you're going to get something back. In business and in marketing, there's an expectation that when you put something (money, time, effort) into it you're going to get something back. But when you have your wires crossed in how you're thinking about it or what you're believing about it, then your results can get crossed and mixed up too.

If you want success in business, you must get to the place where your beliefs and expectations are grounded in God's Truth. It's important that you know who God is and that He intends to provide for you. He owns it all and so you must see this business as His business that you get to steward or manage.

Take a few moments to ask yourself the following questions:

God is a faithful promise keeper. (Hebrews 11 and Hebrews: 10:23) What do I believe about God keeping His promises to me? and to humanity? Do I know what those promises are?

God is my provider. (Matthew 6:8, 32, Luke 12:30, Philippians 4:19, 2 Peter 1:3) What do I believe about His provision?

God is sovereign. (Ephesians 1:17-23) What do I believe about God's sovereignty in regards to my business and marketing results?

For Reflection:

My biggest takeaway from this chapter is....

The truth I need to act on is...

My action will be...

I will take this action on/by (date)...

The earth is the Lord's, and the fulness thereof;
the world, and they that dwell therein.
Psalm 24:1

When a small business grows so that they must hire a CEO (Chief Executive Officer) it's generally because they've reached the point that in order to grow the owner is going to have to give up some of the day to day administration and operations in order to continue being the visionary and director of the company. His time has become too valuable to spend it on the minutiae of administration, marketing and delivery.

The CEO (some also call this person the Integrator) gets hired to both carry out the vision of the owner, (top down) and also to be the buffer between the employees and the owner (bottom up).

The CEO has to know the owner. Know his vision and mission for the business. Know the products, services and transformation the company provides, and in many cases be ready and able to teach and to train in that. He must know the owner's heart for the employees and the clients and customers. Knowing and understanding the end goal, values and standards of the owner are essential in order to manage the company well on his behalf.

As the business develops, the heads of marketing, finance, human resources, and client accounts will all answer to the CEO, who answers to the owner.

And just as a CEO is hired, he can also be fired. This is not his business. The business belongs to the owner. It's the CEO's job to manage, steward, guide, protect, and grow the business. He answers to the owner. And while there is tremendous responsibility in being CEO, there is also freedom.

The owner can still "call the shots". The owner may still have the final say. The owner is still the one ultimately responsible for the company. If revenue is good, the owner is responsible. If the revenue is low, the owner is responsible. The CEO is free to work within his giftings and job description while the final results of the company still lie ultimately with the owner.

Let's take that analogy now and apply it to your business: What would it look like if God were the owner of your business and you were the CEO? What if you let God "fly the plane" and you supported His goals and purposes? That is not only unique in today's society, it also gives you incredible, divine leverage.

Behold, the heaven and the heaven of heavens is the Lord's thy God, the earth also, with all that therein is. Deuteronomy 10:13

Do you believe Deuteronomy 10:13 is talking about your business? If God owns all that is in the earth, doesn't that include "your" business?

If God owns your business, what does that make you?
Ah, yes! The CEO.

Another responsibility of The Owner is that He chooses a CEO. He intentionally asks, invites, chooses, places the CEO into that position. It doesn't happen by accident, but on purpose.

You are the one God chose for this position.

You are the one The Owner chose on purpose for this position, either because He saw in you the potential that could be trained to carry out the position or He'd already pre-qualified you and found you have what it takes. What an amazing, empowering thought!

And in the next chapter you'll discover all the things He says about you that make me 100% certain He thinks you can do this!

For Reflection:

My biggest takeaway from this chapter is....

The truth I need to act on is...

My action will be...

I will take this action on/by (date)...

5. Incredible FAVOR

Behold my servant...in whom my soul delighteth.

Isaiah 42:1

Do you remember the thrill of being a teenager with a crush on someone in your world? Do you remember how your heart felt every time you learned one of your friends had spoken to that person? I suspect your question, like mine, was probably *"What did they say about me?"* And you waited, not daring to breathe, hoping they had said something and that it was even the tiniest bit favorable toward you. And if it was, it gave you confidence. It empowered you to speak and walk and act differently...

A large percentage of the business owners in a recent group I surveyed regarding their struggle to walk out their faith in business said they were struggling with confidence. If you want to be a confident CEO in business, you need to know what the owner says about you.

Isaiah 42:1 says God delights in you. Have you ever thought about God like that, that He delights in you?

Behold my servant, whom I uphold; mine elect, in whom my soul delighteth; I have put my spirit upon him: he shall bring forth judgment to the Gentiles.

And Isaiah 44:24 says that He made you:

Thus saith the Lord, thy redeemer, and he that formed thee from the womb, I am the Lord that maketh all things; that stretcheth forth the heavens alone; that spreadeth abroad the earth by myself;

Isaiah 44:2 says He chose you. He knows you. He will help you:

Thus saith the Lord that made thee, and formed thee from the womb, which will help thee; Fear not, O Jacob, my servant; and thou, Jesurun, whom I have chosen.

Think about a child who draws a picture. They run in excitedly shouting: *"Mommy, mommy, look what I made. Look what I did!"* In my coaching programs we call this being "second grade proud".

The child is showing everyone. They're showing the grandparents and they're getting on zoom to show uncle so-and-so in another city. When Daddy comes in, they run to him to show him too. They insist their artwork gets the place of honor on the refrigerator to continue to show off the glory of their creation. They are so delighted.

I can't help but believe that God delights in you and me in the same way: *"Look what I made! Look at how amazing and unique you are. I delight in you!"*

The Lord hath appeared of old unto me, saying, Yea, I have loved thee with an everlasting love: therefore with lovingkindness have I drawn thee. Jeremiah 31:3

Nay, in all these things we are more than conquerors through him that loved us. For I am persuaded, that neither death, nor life, nor angels, nor principalities, nor powers, nor things present, nor things to come, Nor height, nor depth, nor any other creature, shall be able to separate us from the love of God, which is in Christ Jesus our Lord. Romans 8:37-39

God loves you with incredible favor and eternal love. He made you and called you to fulfill a specific purpose. He wants to put you on display because you bring glory to Him.

Isaiah 42:6 He says:

I the Lord have called thee in righteousness, and will hold thine hand, and will keep thee, and give thee for a covenant of the people, for a light of the Gentiles;

Which brings me to the second thing God says about you: He has a specific purpose for you.

If you're still here, there's still a reason for you to be here.

There's still someone that you need to impact in the world. God has a specific calling for you and of you. And lest you still feel unqualified, He also promises to do through you, what He calls you to do:
Faithful is he that calleth you, who also will do it. 1 Thessalonians 5:24

Finally we see God choosing those who are "filled and skilled" as my friend Matt likes to say.

It is interesting reading through Exodus 28 about those people who were called to work on the things that were going into the building and service of the Tabernacle. God specifically commanded them to engage craftsmen who were also filled with the spirit of wisdom to work at creating garments, and at working with precious stones, gold, silver and brass for the instruments that would be used in the Tabernacle.

And thou shalt speak unto all that are wise hearted, whom I have filled with the spirit of wisdom, that they may make Aaron's garments to consecrate him, that he may minister unto me in the priest's office. Exodus 28:3

He specifically said they were to be wise, filled with the spirit, and skilled in their workmanship.

You have skills. All of us do. God has invested in you a skill and not only are you to be good at your work, but you're to be wise and to be filled with the Spirit because God wants to use you for His work. He promises that when you are willing to be used, He'll actually do the work through you. I can't imagine a better work environment, can you?

For Reflection:

My biggest takeaway from this chapter is....

The truth I need to act on is...

My action will be...

I will take this action on/by (date)...

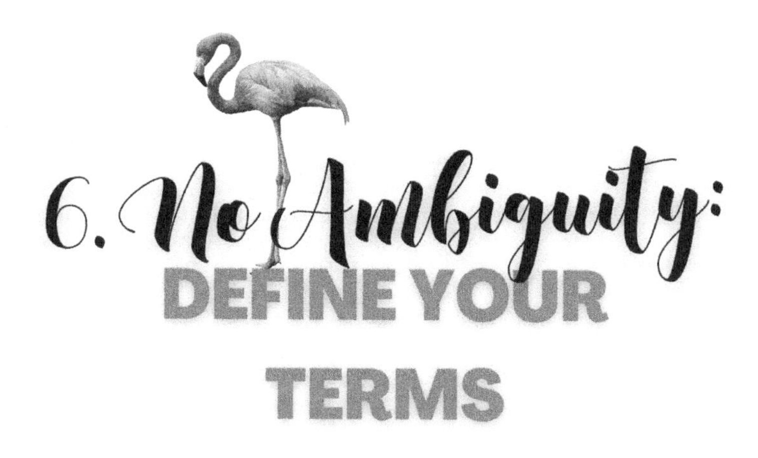

I have no greater joy than that my children walk in truth.

3 John 1:4

I was crushed. I'd just spent 2 days of my life compiling data and statistics, writing scripts and summaries, filming and editing a testimonial video about how the program I'd invested for the past 7 months had helped us reach over 5,000 families in an online training summit. We'd not just served a lot of people, we'd made history in the Spanish-speaking homeschool world, and I just knew we'd make it to the final round!

This contest of sorts was touted to be weighted just as heavily on impact as income, and we'd just changed the lives and futures of nearly 20,000 people as near as I could tell - but my story hadn't made the cut. I'd been rejected.

Success in this instance, I realized, was not just determined by impact, it was six-figures + impact. The lives changed were important, but not as important as making the program look good by highlighting the ones who'd generated lots of revenue.

And that was the day I understood how important it is to define your terms for yourself and for the people you lead (family, team, clients, etc.), and to define them based on God's definitions not man's.

I did eventually hit six-figures and get recognized, but I will never forget that lesson.

My mentor Dan Miller explains it this way in his book *Wisdom Meets Passion*: *"Living large does not necessarily mean a bigger salary, house, cars, or retirement fund. It has nothing to do with fancy vacations or the latest fashions. Rather, it means having a life that is full of meaning and purpose. And that can occur - or be absent - at any place on the continuum of the traditional parameters of success. I've seen millionaires who are living life "small" and those with scarce financial resources who are living "large."*[9]

Money has no value in heaven, my friend. Money = pavement in heaven. (Revelation 21:21) So then why, on earth, would I put an emphasis on heaping up tons of pavement? God says:

I have no greater joy than that my children walk in truth. 3 John 1:4

Wow! That definition of success has nothing to do with a dollar sign! If you think about it, God doesn't even use money. There is no money in heaven. God doesn't need money. He owns everything. (Psalm 24:1)

Money is a tool that we use here on earth, but it means nothing to God outside of its function of provision and stewardship.

Do not lay up for yourselves treasures on earth, where moth and rust destroy and where thieves break in and steal. Matthew 6:19

There is no intrinsic or eternal value in money. So why is it so important to us? Because it's a distraction the enemy uses.

When I dug into God's Word to study more on this topic, I realized that money is not evil in and of itself, a belief I'd been struggling with a lot in ministry where stories of lack and personal sacrifice can nearly deify a person.

God's Word doesn't say money is evil. He says the love of money is where evil takes root (1 Timothy 6:10). The enemy uses a desire in your heart for provision (a good desire) and focuses you on the money (the wrong source) until it becomes a distraction, and in some cases an obsession and an idol. That's what makes it evil. (See also Ezekiel 7:19) When you begin to love money more than God, when you seek money more than you trust God's provision, when you value income more than the lives and success of the people you serve, it becomes evil.

When you have a godly view of money you can see and use money as an incredible tool in God's Kingdom. I mean, think of it; the more money you make, the more impact for good you can have if your heart, your motive, is in the right place.

Let's read God's definition of success again. He says: *I have no greater joy than to hear that my children walk in truth.*

He doesn't say I have no greater joy than that my children have a bank account of X number of dollars. He doesn't say I have no greater joy than that my children are doctors or lawyers or teachers, or professional NFT traders... God says He measures success in that you walk in truth. And who is truth? God is the embodiment of truth.

I am the way, the truth, and the life. John 14:6

He says He is physically the truth. The living truth. So when you walk in truth, you are walking in Him, walking in Christ. That is how God defines success. God also defines a successful person as a teacher.

All of us, regardless of the work we're doing for business, get to teach God's ways and His laws, His truths to other people.

For verily I say unto you, Till heaven and earth pass, one jot or one tittle shall in no wise pass from the law, till all be fulfilled. Whosoever therefore shall break one of these least commandments, and shall teach men so, he shall be called the least in the kingdom of heaven: but whosoever shall do and teach them, the same shall be called great in the kingdom of heaven. Matthew 5:18-19

You are the channel God wants to use to teach His truth to other people. That could be through teaching veterinary skills. That could be through teaching English literature. That could be on a coaching call, at a business event, in a mechanics class, a birthing class, a baking class or a virtual business conference. Wherever you are, He says you will be great in the Kingdom, when you walk in truth and teach His words to other people.

The world equates success with money and possessions. God says seeking Him first means you are successful. He says to seek Him first and you'll have all that other stuff too:

But seek ye first the kingdom of God, and His righteousness; and all these things shall be added unto you. Matthew 6:33.

He's talking about provision, the things you wear and eat. He says not to worry about them, but to seek Him first. Everything that comes after the seeking is the reward. In other words, seek Him, do what He's called you to do, and let Him take care of providing and rewarding.

A CEO who trusts God as provider is never worried about making a sale or earning enough revenue. You should be concerned with doing your job with excellence, making invitations to prospective clients for God's glory, for the good of those you get to serve... God will take care of the revenue.

God says: Apart from me, you can do nothing, John 15:5 and in Matthew 19:26 and Mark 10:27 He says: with God, all things are possible.

So, in order to have God's blessing on your work,
You've got to know Him.

You've got to know what He says about Himself.

You've got to know what He says about you.

You've got to know what He says about success.

Then you've got to align your heart beliefs with what He says. Because that is the truth. And that is the power of the living Word in your life.

When your goals for your business, your desires for the people that you're serving and your own definition of success align with what God says and with His truth, then you will be successful on a day-to-day basis.

Recently Sahra, one of our masterclass[10] students, sent me this message (and gave me permission to share). She said: *"I have not had much financial success in this business - yet, but I've been able to love on people like crazy and God has made me a different person through this business. I've been able to pray with the people I talk to about my offer, encourage them, love on them and share the Gospel with them.*

My brain keeps saying "Where is the financial compensation?" And my heart is in awe saying "Wow! Lord, you just used me to bless them." I don't know what He's doing with the business, but I know this is His version of success, like you've been teaching, and I am ok with that and massively grateful. It's just the strangest feeling. Thank you for your ministry and your business. It's blessed me so much."

Biblical success, success according to God, has not a thing in the world to do with how much money you make or don't make. It has everything to do with how you love God, know God, and love others, as well as how you love how He made you.

And Jesus answered him, The first of all the commandments is, Hear, O Israel; The Lord our God is one Lord: And thou shalt love the Lord thy God with all thy heart, and with all thy soul, and with all thy mind, and with all thy strength: this is the first commandment. And the second is like, namely this, Thou shalt love thy neighbour as thyself. There is none other commandment greater than these.

Mark 12:29-31

For Reflection:

My biggest takeaway from this chapter is....

The truth I need to act on is...

My action will be...

I will take this action on/by (date)...

What does God require of you? But to act justly.
To love mercy, to walk humbly with your God.
Micah 6:8

If God owns everything. This is His business. That's why He's not your CEO. It's not your business. It's His business. He owns it. Everything you own is from Him.

When we left ministry number one and moved across Mexico to Campeche, we arrived with the contents of 15 suitcases to our name. That's it. Everything we owned was in those suitcases and in a few boxes at my parents' house in the States.

Yet everything we have now, a 250-year-old home, more beds than we have people for, furniture in every room, all the dishes and appliances, even down to our 8 passenger van. All of our blessings have been given to us by God. And this business is a blessing from God as well. It's all His, and He can't be the CEO of the business if it's His business to begin with.

Recognizing God as The Owner is key to knowing if the next step is God's direction, or is you devising your own way.

Someone in a marketing class[11] I taught recently asked, *"How do you differentiate between God's step and your own step?"* She said, *"I'll take the step. I just want to be sure that it's God's and not my own."*

The key is to base it off the truth that this is God's business. You've got to know The Owner of the business. He owns it all. It's not your 90% and His 10%, it's His 100%. It's all His, and He lets you manage that 100% as CEO. So knowing your next step means knowing Him well enough to what He would want you to do.

I know a lot of us struggle with feeling that if I do this or that in business, somebody is not going to love me. It's a human need we have for love.

Tap and I struggled with it a lot when we first got started in business because of all those years of ministry under someone else's direction and judgment.

Once we had our own business and only answered to God we had to relearn how to listen to God's voice and guidance to step out and take action with confidence again.

If you're doing what God wants you to do, human disapproval, however distracting, is irrelevant.

God is one million times a better boss than the best human boss you can imagine. God only requires that you walk with Him.

He hath shewed thee, O man, what is good; and what doth the Lord require of thee, but to do justly, and to love mercy, and to walk humbly with thy God? Micah 6:8:

God is your judge. He is your Father. He is your protector. He is your keeper. He is your provider. And when you see things from this perspective it relieves the pressure to people please.

God chose you to be His CEO. He chose *you* for this, not that other person. He's trained you for this through all the work and experiences in your life. He has put you in this position for this time, because He believes you can do this through His strength.

Don't let other people cheat you out of the blessing and the privilege of embracing your place in God's Kingdom. This is God's work and He chose you. He says He has called you to walk with Him. Learn of Him and let Him do the work through you.

Take my yoke upon you, and learn of me; for I am meek and lowly in heart: and ye shall find rest unto your souls. Matthew 11:29.

Faithful is he that calleth you, who also will do it. 1 Thessalonians 5:24

According as his divine power hath given unto us all things that pertain unto life and godliness, through the knowledge of him that hath called us to glory and virtue. 2 Peter 1:3

When He says you have "everything you need for life and godliness," business falls under the life category.

How do you have everything you need? Through knowing Him, who has called you "according to His glory and excellence."

You're not to worry. Matthew 6 has multiple verses that tell us not to be concerned about what comes tomorrow. God is already in tomorrow (Hebrews 13:8). He already knows. He is the owner of this company. He is responsible for it. You can trust Him.

And once you begin to trust Him, and stop worrying about upsetting others, you begin to walk in relationship with Him and know His expectations for you, that brings freedom!

God doesn't just want you to know Him. He wants you to hear His voice. John 10:27 says:

My sheep hear my voice and I know them. They follow me. I give unto them eternal life.

In chapter 13 of *Faith Like Flamingos*[12], I shared about the flamingo's unique voice or unique chirp or tweet or whatever you want to call it. It's unique to each individual bird. When the parents leave the baby flamingo in flamingo daycare, go off to find food and come back for him, that unique call is how they find their baby. The baby knows this is my mom or my dad when it hears their voice. How cool is that?

To know the owner of the company, you need more than knowledge of Him. You also need to know Him, be receptive to His voice. There must be a relationship there, and that relationship allows you to know what He expects for His business.

When you are the CEO of God's business, it takes a lot of pressure off because the buck stops with The Owner. The CEO takes directions from The Owner. The CEO is in charge of a lot of the operation and administration, but the ultimate, last and final word is for The Owner. So if God is The Owner, it creates freedom and so much less stress. Because now when you face a decision, you just have to ask if God would want it and the answer becomes clear.

Asking these three questions helps me determine if something is the right idea at the right time:

1. Is this in alignment with God's goals for our company right now?
2. Would God be pleased with this?
3. Would this make God look good?

If you're the owner, all the stress and pressure is on you to decide. But if you're the CEO and managing this for The Owner, then all you have to do is be in alignment with The Owner by knowing and understanding what He wants. Your job is to do what He wants. I don't know about you, but I get excited about being CEO because being an owner is the tougher job.

Let God be The Owner. Endeavor to embrace your place as CEO. Then be the best CEO you can be.

Nobody would ever walk into a company and say, *"Hey, I'm here to be your CEO!"* without having been intentionally and thoughtfully invited to the position.

Likewise, no one ever takes a position as CEO of any kind of company without knowing exactly what that job description is and first understanding what is expected.

As the CEO you have a choice to accept or reject the position. God is not forcing this on you.

There are numerous examples in Scripture of people who felt less than qualified and God reassured them that He was with them and indeed wanted them for the job:

- Noah (Genesis 6-7)
- Moses (Exodus 4)
- Joshua (Joshua 1)
- Gideon (Judges 6-7)

- Esther (Esther 4)
- Nehemiah (Nehemiah 1-2)
- Peter (John 21)
- Ananias (Acts 9)

And so many more...

What does God expect of a CEO? Let's go back to His Word...

What does God require of you? But to act justly. To love mercy, to walk humbly with your God. Micah 6:8

Notice, none of that said earn seven-figures a year. God says, I require that you...

- Act justly.
- Love mercy.
- Walk with me.
- Be humble.
- Obeying my voice (Jeremiah 18:9-10),
- Love one another (John 13:34, 15:12),
- Use your gifts for the benefit of the whole body of Christ (Romans 12),
- Invest wisely (Proverbs 21:5, 20),
- Be generous by selling to others the materials they need (Proverbs 11:26, 2 Corinthians 9:6, Luke 6:39)
- Do everything you do for my glory (1 Corinthians 10:31).

All of these things are straight from God's Word and tell you how to do the job of running a business.

Thus saith the Lord, Let not the wise man glory in his wisdom, neither let the mighty man glory in his might, let not the rich man glory in his riches: But let him that glorieth glory in this, that he understandeth and knoweth me, that I am the Lord which exercise lovingkindness, judgment, and righteousness, in the earth: for in these things I delight, saith the Lord. Jeremiah 9:23-24

The glory (which can mean honor, reward or to take pride in[13]) comes in knowing God and in doing what He created you to do. In John 6:38 Jesus said, *"I am come to do the will of Him that sent me."*

And what is the will of God? To serve, to love, to tell of Jesus, to use your gifts.

Nowhere in Scripture does God command you to make a ton of money for money hoarding sake. In fact, the opposite is true: you find commands to be generous and to sell your crops (Proverbs 11:26).

Nowhere in Scripture do you find instruction to have a retirement account of a million dollars. You do see a command to provide for your family (1 Timothy 5:8). Millions may come as a reward and as a blessing, once you prove you can handle God's blessings, but that's not a guarantee.

What God does guarantee is peace in the work, because success on a daily basis comes from walking with Him and doing what He asks of you as the CEO (Romans 2:10), not from finances or material wealth.

God wants you to enjoy the work

He's called you to.

There is nothing better for a person than that he should eat and drink and find enjoyment in his toil. This also, I saw, is from the hand of God.
Ecclesiastes 2:24 ESV

And He wants you to be faithful.

Moreover it is required in stewards, that a man be found faithful.
I Corinthians 4:2

There is no CEO in the world who can wake up with a 10 o'clock appointment, and just go back to bed and oversleep because they just didn't feel like getting there, without risking the position. When you are CEO of God's work, you must take the job seriously.

The business God has placed you in charge of may be a full-time job for you. Or it may be part-time or a second job. Whatever God is giving you to do, you need to take the work seriously. Show up, work the hours you set and keep appointments, even if they are with yourself. You can't just say *"I didn't feel like it today."* There are consequences in any business for not showing up, and God's business is no different.

Why would it be okay when you're working for God, but not when you're working for a human? You've got to show up and do the work. It's called commitment and as my mentor Bari Baumgardner[14] is so fond of saying: To be successful, *"You must choose commitment over convenience."*

You must choose commitment over convenience.

The soul of the sluggard desireth, and hath nothing: but the soul of the diligent shall be made fat. Proverbs 13:4

Personal accountability is very important. If you mess up, own it. Communication with The Owner is like any other: *"I messed up. How do I make it right, God?"*

These are things that a CEO does, taking responsibility for his own actions and for the people under him.

And how does this apply to marketing you may be asking? Everything here applies to marketing because everything you do and say becomes a piece of a marketing strategy which reflects the quality (or lack thereof) of your brand, products, courses and programs. If these foundational beliefs and practices are not in place, the best marketing in the world will not help you sustain success for any length of time.

For Reflection:

My biggest takeaway from this chapter is....

The truth I need to act on is...

My action will be...

I will take this action on/by (date)...

8. Origin VS. RESOURCES

That unto every one which hath shall be given; and from him that hath not, even that he hath shall be taken away from him.

Luke 19:26

I was pretty impressed with myself about the new swimming hole my cousins and I had created in the stream down the hill from my grandparents house. As a kid in the mountains of western North Carolina, there was nothing so glorious as a day spent catching crawdads or architecting the flow of water into a 2-3 foot deep pool we could splash and play in imagining ourselves to be explorers on all kinds of dangerous adventures. Today was going to be a hot one and I couldn't wait to finish my homework and get back to the creek.

My glory was a bit short lived however, because when I arrived I didn't find a clear, refreshing mountain pool at all. The force of the water from the rains over the weekend had weakened our rooky dam and all our hard work had been destroyed. The shallow stream was as clear - and shallow - as always. I learned later that dams built by professionals have spillways that allow excess water to overflow so that the pent up pressure doesn't damage the structure. For a reservoir to be healthy and safe, there has to be inflow and outflow.

This came back to me the other day as I was thinking about how a healthy business has both inflow and outflow. My friend Samantha[15] frequently reminds me that God intends for us to *"be the Sea of Galilee both receiving in and flowing out"* because if we just receive and don't share we become like the *"stinky Dead Sea."*

Christian author Shae Bynes[16] has a habit of saying *"God is the source. Everything else is a resource."* Both of these sayings bear tremendous truth for the resources and the finances (including marketing budgets) of a business.

There are many resources in a business. They may be in the form of people, of digital and physical assets, of time, of expertise or advice, and of money. We must bear in mind that all of these originate with God, who is the source. He created it all. He owns it all and He is not broke, and if we hoard those resources or misuse them, it can create stink and damage.

Your job as CEO is to steward the resources you've received into the best use to meet The Owner's goals for the company. Knowing God, knowing what He wants for you, and knowing what He wants for the business allows you to have the confidence to make resource decisions with ease and in alignment with His goals.

Then when you're presented with an opportunity, you can say, *"all right, this is the goal I know God has set before me for this time. Does this opportunity get me closer to that goal?"* And if it does, great, go there. If it doesn't, then this is not for you, or this is not the right time to pursue that opportunity.

When you know the goal, you can more easily discern if an opportunity will get you closer to that goal and the whole process is simplified. It's not emotional. It's factual, based on the goals that God has set before you. (More on this in chapter 20). This makes decision making much easier, less stressful, and allows you to have a clear answer almost immediately.

For example: when we knew our main goal for the quarter was to generate leads for our business and we were presented with an opportunity to speak on a podcast or summit or to sponsor an event, we could ask the question "*How does this help us reach our goal of getting leads?*" If it did, it was something we could discuss in more detail, if it didn't, we could immediately table it for a future discussion and not be distracted by it right now.

Do you have policies and procedures in place to protect the various resources of God's business?

Human resources are often the easiest to align by asking if the person has the knowledge, time and skill set to do the job at hand? You might also need to ask if they share your values and understand and support your stated goals.

A lot of marketing instruction talks about giving stuff away: free content, free consults, free information... Time resources are often the easiest to manipulate, yet the hardest to make up if wasted. And you have to answer for financial resources too. The gurus will tell you it's good marketing, and while you do want to always be serving your people with value, you must be very careful.

If the giving is not in alignment with the goals of The Owner and the policies of the company, it becomes either theft or fraud.

In order to be clear on God's goals for your generosity you need to be clear on what God wants of you. You've also got to have policies and procedures in place to protect the objective. It's awesome to give things to people who really have a hard time and need what you have to offer, if God's putting that on your heart. As the trusted CEO He installed in this position, you have the prerogative to make that decision. But consistently giving away products and services that are eating into profits, can escalate quickly into a very serious problem.

To protect the profits it is imperative to talk to God about the policies and procedures you have in place. This process and the end result will look different for each CEO as the Holy Spirit puts on each heart how to manage His business.

For a solopreneur, a written policy might be just on the computer, or on a website. Maybe it's just between you, your partner and God right now, but somewhere you need a written policy that says what you will and will not do so it can ground and guide you in the emotional moment. For a larger business it becomes part of your operating procedures or company handbook.

Having parameters around the giving protects the assets and future growth ability of the business. It's not just willy-nilly whenever somebody pulls your heartstrings. You actually have a pattern and a policy that can wisely guide the decision so those heartstrings aren't just taking over emotionally. Emotional giving will ruin the business profits, and your ability to grow and reach more and more people.

Here's are two example giving policies:

1. We will give one class away for every ten classes sold.
2. For every twenty coaching packages sold, we'll give a partial scholarship to someone who applies and qualifies.

Remember, money is just a tool. This is not about making money. This is about how to help the business grow and reach more people with the message that God has asked you to give. That usually involves some sort of financial involvement. If a business is not covering cost, it's a hobby, not a business. If you're giving all the finances away, it'll be nearly impossible to reach people.

It's also about helping people value what they receive. In general, people will pay better attention and apply themselves better when it costs them something.

Applying logic is important, as well as some financial savvy. Again, God has given you everything you need for life and godliness (2 Peter 1:3). If you lack training in this area, God's provided it (James 1:5). There are books, courses, and mentors to help you gain proficiency. You need to ask yourself what you need to learn next to be the best CEO of the business resources God has entrusted to you.

When you have well structured policies and procedures, you have clarity and confidence to make every decision easily because you're clear on God's goals and you'll be able to meet those goals while making a bigger impact in the Kingdom.

Being in alignment with God will give you peace on a day-to-day basis. That's going to give you joy. That's going to make you wake up, like I do, excited every day about who I get to help today. I have peace becauseI'm doing what I know He wants me to do each day. With clarity in deciding my next steps, it's easy to make decisions by simply asking, *"Does this work with what God wants? Yes or no?"* No emotion involved.

This is not a prosperity gospel. I am not saying if you do this, you will get that. It's not about you, and getting more for you. This is not about getting rich so you can retire in a mansion and eat doughnuts all day. This is not an, if you do A, God will B.

God is God. He can do whatever He wants and He is the source of all things. There is no magic formula for getting what you want out of Him. It's about faith and trust in Him to guide and direct you for His glory.

This is about serving Him out of a heart of gratitude. This is, *"Lord. I don't deserve anything. Everything you've given is completely from your favor. It's your complete graciousness in my life. What can I do to serve you?"*

When you have that heart, when you have a heart that is walking after righteousness, that is the heart God will bless.

You have His complete favor. There is no way in the world God could love you any more than He already does right now. But He wants so much more for you in terms of your impact for Him in the world.

When you recognize Him as the origin of the favor and the resources you also see Him as the One in charge of the results.

My family and I worked seven years of Sundays and Wednesday nights and Saturday Bible clubs and extra activities to plant a church for God in southern México. We witnessed a couple of salvations in that amount of time but the work never grew into a full congregation.

To the rest of the world it looked like a failure, but you know what? God kept reminding us that He didn't call us to do the "saving." He called us to do the work. Over and over He impressed upon our discouraged hearts, *"You be faithful with what I've called you to do, and leave the results up to me."*

And let us not be weary in well doing: for in due season we shall reap, if we faint not. Galatians 6:9

You have His complete favor. There is no way in the world God could love you any more than He already does right now. But He wants so much more for you in terms of your impact for Him in the world.

God provides the results. He asks you to be willing to do the work, to get the message out, and to love the people. Knowing Him is key to all of this. Communication with Him is key to knowing how He wants you to serve people, and how He wants you to love them.

So if you're thinking right now that you could accept this position as CEO of God's business, I want you to write it down somewhere, right here in this book, or in a Bible or journal:

"I accept the position of CEO."
I'm willing to be God's CEO.
I'll let Him guide the business.
I'll do what He says.
I'll listen. I'll know Him. I'll walk with Him.
I'll get clear on what He wants from me.
I accept the position of CEO."

For Reflection:

My biggest takeaway from this chapter is....

The truth I need to act on is...

My action will be...

I will take this action on/by (date)...

"CHRISTIANITY IS EITHER RELEVANT ALL THE TIME OR USELESS ANY TIME."

RICHARD C. HALVERSON

PART TWO

STAY *Relevant*

THE 8 GREATEST MYTHS ABOUT CHRISTIAN MARKETING AND THE TRUTHS THAT GIVE YOU VICTORY

You may be like I was several years ago and just waking up to the fact that you have been believing lies from other people, from the world, and even lies you created in your own head about how business and marketing should or shouldn't be.

There are four things that need to happen to gain victory...

1. You've got to recognize the lies that do not align with the truth of God's Word.
2. You must repent and ask the Lord's forgiveness for believing and acting on those things that you now know were not true.
3. You must restate your belief in the truth. Meditate on the truth to replace the old thought patterns in your brain.
4. You must take new action based on truth.

Maybe you didn't know that it wasn't true until now. If the Holy Spirit has revealed to you that there is truth that needs to replace that, then now is the time to say, *"Lord, forgive me for not seeking your truth, for not evaluating this against your Word, help me see Your truth and act on that in my life."*

The whole of part two is dedicated to exposing the lies we've been believing about God and our ourselves and business and replacing it with God's Truth.

#HUMORUSCO

9. Myth #1

MIXING FAITH AND BUSINESS RENDERS YOU IRRELEVANT, AND OFFENSIVE

Shew me thy faith without thy works,
and I will shew thee my faith by my works.
James 2:18

"You shouldn't mention your faith or talk about God so much. You're going to push people away and it'll stunt your business growth."

For a minute I couldn't even respond to my new assistant's comment. It was still early in our business and the thought that faith might be an obstacle to growth had not crossed my mind before. But that day, I made a choice. I was not going to leave God out of my business. In the end, it was the assistant and I who parted ways.

I have continued to be true to my Lord as I run this business. I'm not obnoxious about my faith. I don't force my beliefs on the people I interact with. I don't belittle others if their ideas don't match mine, but I am confident in who I am in Christ and I know I cannot separate that from what I do. What's more, God has raised me up as a teacher and an encourager to other believers in business who want to know how to walk in alignment with their faith while also successful in life and business.

Like Paul, I say: *For I am not ashamed of the gospel, because it is the power of God that brings salvation to everyone who believes: first to the Jew, then to the Gentile.* Romans 1:16

In chapter 1 of *Faith Like Flamingos*[17], I mentioned the fact that the flamingo is pink all the way through. It's not just their feathers. Their skin, tissues, blood and even their milk is pink. You can't take the pink out of the bird.

Likewise, I don't believe you can take your identity as a child of God out of you. The flamingo doesn't set aside his pinkness to go look for food or build a nest and put it back on when he comes back to the flock. And neither can you set aside who you are on the inside while you do certain activities in life. Your faith goes with you no matter where you go or what you do.

When you see business and marketing through the lens of God's bigger story, much is put into perspective.

When you see every transaction as an opportunity to love a soul created by God, it becomes much more interesting. When you see customer service and public relations as a tool with which you can glorify God or defame Him, the course of action is more clear. When you see stewardship of resources as a way to impact more people in the Kingdom, it becomes less of a chore and more of an exciting challenge.

And you may find that even a gentle faith offends. There were even people who were offended with Jesus (Matthew 13:57, 26:31).

Blessed are they which are persecuted for righteousness' sake: for theirs is the kingdom of heaven. Blessed are ye, when men shall revile you, and persecute you, and shall say all manner of evil against you falsely, for my sake. Rejoice, and be exceeding glad: for great is your reward in heaven: for so persecuted they the prophets which were before you. Matthew 5:10-12

In my experience, those who have been offended by faith have generally had an unpleasant encounter with a professing child of God who was not choosing to act in alignment with God's truth, or they've already personally rejected God's truth. And while that's unfortunate, their response is not your responsibility.

It's not your responsibility (or mine) to pass judgment on them, other than to inspect their fruit for proof of salvation (John 13:35). But for the grace of God, that could be your situation. (1 Timothy 1:15).

It's also not your responsibility to defend the one who offended them. That's between them and God. It is your responsibility to love God, show God's love to others and give God a good name in everything you do.

And thou shalt love the Lord thy God with all thy heart, and with all thy soul, and with all thy mind, and with all thy strength: this is the first commandment. And the second is like, namely this, Thou shalt love thy neighbour as thyself. There is none other commandment greater than these. Mark 12:30-31

In all things shewing thyself a pattern of good works: in doctrine shewing uncorruptness, gravity, sincerity, sound speech, that cannot be condemned; that he that is of the contrary part may be ashamed, having no evil thing to say of you. Titus 2:7-8

Whether therefore ye eat, or drink, or whatsoever ye do, do all to the glory of God. 1 Corinthians 10:31

That part gets me every time, because "whatsoever ye do" includes business activities, customer interactions and marketing the business - it includes all of the business.

For Reflection:

My biggest takeaway from this chapter is....

The lie I have been believing is...

The truth I need to believe and act on is...

My action will be...

I will take this action on/by (date)...

10. Myth #2

YOU CAN'T CHARGE BECAUSE YOU'RE A CHRISTIAN

He that withholdeth corn, the people shall curse him:
but blessing shall be upon the head of him that selleth it.
Proverbs 11:26

Kathy is a gifted Christian coach for women who've experienced traumatic loss. She's also a pastor's daughter, married a pastor, lost a child through a traumatic accident and lived her whole life in service to others.[18]

During our weekly client mastermind call Kathy shared how she'd opened up to a friend about one of the new programs she's putting together for her clients, and how her excitement was dashed when that friend remarked *"Oh Kathy, you're not one of those girls who charge that much."*

The gasp around the zoom room was seen more than heard as we all physically reacted to those words being spoken to someone we all know is worth a crazy amount more than her pricing reflects.

And to her credit Kathy responded with *"No, I AM that girl. I have always been that girl. I've just never charged what she's worth. Until now."*

Value is relevant. Something is only worth what another person is willing to give in exchange for it. And when you believe the lie that a Christian must give everything away, you devalue His name, His excellence and His ability to work His will and His power through you.

There are many verses in Scripture that speak to charging for your work. The Bible directs us in selling ethically and justly, while paying the necessary taxes and even the applicable customs fees.

For the Scripture saith, thou shalt not muzzle the ox that treadeth out the corn. And, The labourer is worthy of his reward. 1 Timothy 5:18

He that withholdeth corn, the people shall curse him: but blessing shall be upon the head of him that selleth it. Proverbs 11:26

Ye shall do no unrighteousness in judgment, in meteyard, in weight, or in measure. Just balances, just weights, a just ephah, and a just hin, shall ye have: I am the Lord your God, which brought you out of the land of Egypt. Therefore shall ye observe all my statutes, and all my judgments, and do them: I am the Lord. Leviticus 19:35-37

Render therefore to all their dues: tribute to whom tribute is due; custom to whom custom; fear to whom fear; honour to whom honour. Romans 13:7 (read vs 1-8. See also Matthew 17:24-27, 22:15-21).

And there are numerous examples of believers in the Bible who ran businesses:

- Abraham, Isaac, Jacob, and Esau all had flocks and herds. (Genesis)
- King David's father owned flocks and herds. (1 Samuel 17:15)
- Boaz and Ruth were corn farmers. (Ruth 2)
- Gideon was a wheat farmer. (Judges 6:11)
- Joseph and Jesus were carpenters. (Matthew 13:55, Mark 6:3)
- Several of the disciples were fishermen. (Matthew 4:19, Mark 1:17)
- Lydia made and sold purple cloth. (Acts 16)
- Luke was a (hired) physician. (Colossians 4:14)
- Paul made and sold tents. (Acts 18)
- Priscilla and Aquila were tent makers. (Acts 18)

And so many more!

There is overwhelming biblical evidence in favor of selling with integrity. There is also great evidence in favor of generosity and caring for the poor, but never in the context of putting one's own business or livelihood at risk. Even the precedent of the tithe in Leviticus 27 was given out of abundance, not out of scarcity.

One of my coaches is fond of saying: *"When you do well, you can do good."* Meaning, the more money you accumulate as a tool in exchange for the value of your knowledge, services and products, the more of that tool you have in hand to grow the work God has entrusted to you. According to the parable of the talents in Matthew 25, the more you steward well, the more you can be entrusted to manage.

For unto every one that hath shall be given, and he shall have abundance: but from him that hath not shall be taken away even that which he hath. Mathew 25:29

For Reflection:

My biggest takeaway from this chapter is....

The lie I have been believing is...

The truth I need to believe and act on is...

My action will be...

I will take this action on/by (date)...

11. Myth #3

CHRISTIAN BUSINESS MEANS SELLING CHRISTIAN-THEMED MERCHANDISE

By this shall all men know that ye are my disciples,
if ye have love one to another.
John 13:35

You have only to run an internet search for "Christian quotes merchandise" to quickly discover that there are many secular companies selling Christian-themed merchandise. It's obviously not a value for them based on the other things they sell, it's simply a profitable marketing niche.

Selling Christian-themed products does not make your business a Christian business, any more than regularly visiting a building designated as a place of worship makes you a Christian. To be a Christian there must be beliefs and actions supporting those beliefs.

That if thou shalt confess with thy mouth the Lord Jesus, and shalt believe in thine heart that God hath raised him from the dead, thou shalt be saved. Romans 10:9

On the other side of this logical argument, there are also many businesses owned and operated by believers whose products and marketing do not explicitly state their beliefs or quote Scripture, but they are not "secular" businesses.

In his book *The Marketplace Christian*[19], Darren Shearer says:
"In most parts of the world, people who identify as Christians represent a massive percentage of the population, so it makes good business sense to have Christ-centered companies serving an explicitly "Christian" market by providing Christian-themed goods and services. In fact, the book you are reading now is Christian-themed. At the same time, we are called to disciple entire industries. This will require that we, as Christians in the marketplace, set our sights on broader market shares than merely those that are explicitly Christian-themed."

So if the product sold doesn't make your business Christian, what does?

Your beliefs, vision, mission, values and actions set you apart. The policies, excellence, and experience your business provides clearly identify you as a secular or Christ-centered business.

The way you and your team speak, work, act and engage with each other, your clients and the public also very clearly shows where your beliefs lie.

A new commandment I give unto you, That ye love one another; as I have loved you, that ye also love one another. By this shall all men know that ye are my disciples, if ye have love one to another. John 13:34-35

So, you might ask, *"Katie, If I am a believer with a bakery, or a Christian teaching music, mechanics, or accounting classes... Does that mean that my products and marketing have to have Bible verses plastered all over them?"*

The answer is no, not necessarily. One way to show Jesus in your business is to serve with care and excellence and another is to show love.

Our eldest daughter has a hobby business making cakes and cookies for sale. She doesn't have to have Scripture verses on those baked goods. She can show the Gospel by having a good attitude, showing respect and love to her customers. Her customer service is prompt, returning phone calls quickly and working with customers in a kind and gracious way.

Two of our daughters are artists.[20] Does that mean their art has to be explicitly religious art in order to be used by God? No, God created everything. He used a burning bush and a talking donkey to give His message (Exodus 3, Numbers 22)... Don't you think He can use the art, products, courses and services He's inspired you to create to give someone a message they need to hear?

The Holy Spirit works in amazing ways. We just need to be willing for Him to do that work. However, if the Holy Spirit is pressing you to be more visible about your beliefs in business, then do it. The key is knowing Him, walking with Him to know when, where and how He wants you to love His people and give His message of salvation, redemption and hope. The love you show, the excellence of your products, courses and services, will open the door for those Kingdom conversations to happen.

The greatest of these is charity (love in action). 1 Corinthians 13:13

I know you might be thinking *"But I don't know how much to show my faith in my business. I understand the Bible verses on the cookies thing. What if I have something else? How much do I talk about my faith? Or how much do I need to make it obvious and blatant in my business?"*

There is no hard fast rule for this. It's going to be different for everyone as you follow the Holy Spirit and let Him guide you and tell you how much. You've got to talk with Him, to seek His glory. Let Him show you. Ask for His wisdom. He'll show you. He'll guide you into all truth (John 16:13).

My friend Matt Tommey, an artist and mentor of Christian artists said, *"I was so worried about what to do when people come into my art studio. I would ask God, 'What do I do, God? Do I need to just drop everything and go witness to them? Because I want to be back over here, making art.' He said, it was like God told him, 'You just need to love the people and let me change the people.' And He said, "I truly believe that God's Holy Spirit is powerful enough to speak through my baskets and sculptures and to heal them or to otherwise influence their lives."*[21]
Faithful is He that calleth you who also will do it. 1 Thessalonians 5:24

God can work through inanimate things. God can work through art He inspires. He can work through food showing His love. He can work through the patience and sweet spirit of a mechanic. He can work through online teachers and coaches.

Let Him work. Don't put limits on how the Holy Spirit can use you. Let God do the work through you His way and in His time.

For Reflection:

My biggest takeaway from this chapter is....

The lie I have been believing is...

The truth I need to believe and act on is...

My action will be...

I will take this action on/by (date)...

12. Myth #4

CHRISTIAN BUSINESS MEANS YOU CAN'T SERVE NON-CHRISTIANS

And he said unto them, Go ye into all the world,
and preach the Gospel to every creature.
Mark 16:15

Pardon the southern expression, but the idea of some believers that you will somehow soil yourself or your reputation if you interact with or serve non-believers is simply hogwash.

"What if God asked me to serve someone who I know is in sin?" Well, my goodness! Do you think God would ask you to show His love to somebody who is in sin? I mean, where do we see that in Scripture?

I'm being a bit facetious here because in Scripture, Jesus Himself set the precedent of showing love to people in sin over and over again...

- To the woman at the well (John 4),
- To the woman caught in adultery (John 8),
- To the lepers (Luke 17)
- To Zacchaeus (Luke 19),

- To Saul (Acts 9)

And to so many more!

What about you and me? We were in sin before He saved us. He showed His love to us. Why would we refuse to show His love to someone who is in sin? Your sin is no different. There are no grade reports on your sin level. Every single sin is just as stinky and appalling in the nose of God as any other sin.

You and I are no better than they, and yet God did not refuse His love or redemption to us. How could you not serve them and show His love to them over and over and over?

So many times Christian business owners say things like *"What if I don't agree? What if I don't like the way they live? How can I serve them?"*

You can serve them because God served you and you may be the only person who shows them the love of Jesus. How cool would that be? What if you loved them and you got a chance to share Jesus with them and He changed their life?!

Jesus wasn't worried about his reputation as He openly served sinners. He prioritized the souls of others over His own reputation.

Loving the non-believer

is not just a marketing choice.

It's a life and death matter.

There are lots of people who refuse to serve others. You don't answer for them, but you do answer for you. The greatest commandments of Jesus were not to shun, shame or convict others, but to love them. You have been called to love as Jesus loves.

This is my commandment, that you love one another as I have loved you.
John 15:12

You may argue: *"But Katie, that verse is talking about loving other believers. These people are not brothers or sisters in Christ."* And I will answer *'They're not a believer - yet."*

Jesus didn't love the sin, that is clear in Scripture, but He never refused to love the person who sinned, including you. God loved us into a relationship with Himself and He wants to do that with the people your business touches too.

I have been to many secular business events in our years of business. Some of them really high ticket events with CEOs of million dollar companies in attendance, and at every single one there have been Kingdom conversation opportunities–sometimes multiple opportunities. People will come up to me and say, *"What is it about you? You just radiate light."* or *"I walked by you and just felt this peace. Why is that?"*

It opens the door to tell them, *"It's Jesus. Do you know who He is? Can I tell you about Him?"*

I have shared Christ with agnostics and seekers, start up founders and millionaires, wait staff and witch doctors... Can you imagine being at a secular, professional event, having a chance to ask someone how their business is doing and see God turn it into a witnessing opportunity because you showed a genuine interest and because you know God loves that individual?

It excites me to think of the potential for the Kingdom walking around at some of these events. If these people are doing this well in their own wisdom, imagine what could happen if God got ahold of their hearts!

This is how you, as a believer, make an impact in the marketplace, by doing what you do well. Shining your light authentically (not obnoxiously) everywhere you go by being sensitive to the Holy Spirit's prompting when those Kingdom conversation opportunities arise. They're not going to know Him if you refuse to engage with them. And if you blend in while engaging, how will they *see* your light and note the difference?

I the Lord have called thee in righteousness, and will hold thine hand, and will keep thee, and give thee for a covenant of the people, for a light of the Gentiles. Isaiah 42:6

And ye shall be witnesses unto me both in Jerusalem, and in all Judaea, and in Samaria, and unto the uttermost part of the earth. Acts 1:8

If you are that one person who stands out because you will love them and serve them because God loves them, you will earn a chance to talk to them about the most important thing in their life - eternal life. That brings glory to God and gives The Owner a good name.

God doesn't place any extraordinary emphasis on profits. He owns it ALL... He values people. Remember, money is just a tool to Him. Money is something that allows you to do more and reach more people so you can share His message with more people.

"But Katie," you say, *"What if there are situations where you truly believe that you cannot serve someone or that you cannot offer a service in good conscience?"* (And I do think sometimes there are situations like that.) I believe the Holy Spirit is there to give you wisdom. If you will think about this in advance, put wise policies in place in your business, and give yourself time to get to know clients and their situations, the Holy Spirit can help you figure out ways to still bless them even while kindly refusing something that goes against His principles or laws.

Perhaps He will allow a schedule conflict to arise. There may be someone else who could better serve the client. Blessing them may look like *"I can't do this right now, but how else can I serve you? If it's not me, then who can I recommend to you?"* The Holy Spirit is there to give wisdom so that even as you're obeying Him you're also not offending. You're not burning any bridges that might prohibit you from reaching them with the Gospel in the future.

God is using people just like you, in all kinds of different niches, interests and talents to reach people all over the world. One of my mastermind clients, Rachel, is a professional quilter[22], with numerous contacts due to the online classes she teaches. During the course of our program she was so excited to share about an opportunity she had to lead an overseas business contact to the Lord. The opportunity came through a casual conversation, about business, and because she was open to using her business as a ministry tool and serving even non-believers. She not only grew her business, but also the Kingdom! He wants to do the same with you.

The Greatest Salesman in the World[23] is an excellent book for Christians in business, and it's one of the texts I most recommend for marketing. One of the main themes in the book is love for your customers. Chapter nine opens with: *"I will greet this day with love in my heart. They may refuse to buy from me, but I will show them love. They may refuse my speech, they may refuse my dress. They may not like the way that I talk or offer things or what I do, but they cannot refuse the love that shines through me."*

That, my friend, is how you bring Christ authentically into the marketplace. Your willingness to love other people sets you apart and makes you unique. God wants you to love and serve others because He is the ultimate example of that love and service.

You don't have to love what they do. You don't have to love what they stand for. You don't have to love what they are or what they promote in their personal life. But you do need to show the love of Christ that says, *"I'm not your judge. I'm just here to support you and help you take the next right step. How can I help?"* This is the kind of uniqueness that changes lives and businesses.

For Reflection:

My biggest takeaway from this chapter is....

The lie I have been believing is...

The truth I need to believe and act on is...

My action will be...

I will take this action on/by (date)...

13. Myth #5

BUSINESS AND MINISTRY MUST BE SEPARATE

Whether therefore ye eat or drink or whatsoever ye do
Do all to the glory of God.
1 Corinthians 10:31

When we began our online business we were missionaries trying to build a business in our "spare time". We withstood storms of comments from well meaning folks about business not "counting" as ministry and questioning whether we were turning our backs on God's calling in order to make money. It would have seemed that ministry was the "highest calling" and we were somehow letting God and others down to downgrade ourselves to working a business.

And yet, Tap and I knew that God was the one leading us into business. We knew He wanted to provide for our family through business, and we have been amazed at the amount of ministry opportunities the Lord has opened to us because of and through the vehicle of our business. We have come to realize that doing what God created you and called you to do is your sacred calling and can be the highest form of worship to your Creator.

Spiritual Gifts are not relegated only to ministry work. The gifting you have was given you to use in whatever work God designed you for and called you to do.

Prior to enrolling in our *Doing Business with God*™ program, Alyssa[24] had a thriving virtual assistant business. She shared how awful she felt, like somehow she was letting God down by not being in a traditional, full-time ministry.

Alyssa said, *"I was trying to please everybody. Through the Doing Business With God coaching experience, I realized I don't have to change my life to have a ministry. My business is ministry too."*

My friend, whatever God has called you to is your best worship. That is your ministry. That's the way He's going to reach the world through you, through the different ways that you touch people who need Him.

I have received message after message while teaching this material in which students said things like, *"You know, I thought I had to wait for a sign from God,"* or *"I thought that what I was doing wasn't sacrificial enough to count as service."*

My answer is, God says He created you just the way you are with these talents and gifts to use for Him! When you understand that, then you realize whatever He has called you to do is your best worship. There is no need to wait for a further sign! Get going!

You can have a full-time ministry while creating artwork for sale.
You can have a full-time ministry while doing life, trauma or career coaching.
You can have a full-time ministry while baking cakes, pies or cookies.
You can have a full-time ministry while driving a delivery truck or taxi service.
You can have a full-time ministry while caring for toddlers or teaching children.
You can have a full-time ministry while teaching online courses.
Hear me when I say this:

Doing what God has created and called you to do is your *best* worship!

Anything that God has called you to do specifically for Him is a full-time ministry because that is the channel He has chosen through which you have access to people, and people are what God cares about. His priority is not the money in your bank account, the house you have or the car you drive. His priority is people!

I am come that they might have life, and that they might have it more abundantly.
John 10:10

This is not a prosperity gospel. You're not to do good work so you can get anything. You do good out of extreme gratitude because you deserve nothing of the goodness He has showered upon your life. The good you do is out of gratefulness to the One who saved you, adopted you, made you new, and gave you His name and inheritance.

For as many as are led by the Spirit of God, they are the sons of God. For ye have not received the spirit of bondage again to fear; but ye have received the Spirit of adoption, whereby we cry, Abba, Father. The Spirit itself beareth witness with our spirit, that we are the children of God. Romans 8:14-16

Therefore if any man be in Christ, he is a new creature: old things are passed away; behold, all things are become new. 2 Corinthians 5:17

Another one of our students, Angela[25] said, *"I have been so encouraged to see my business as God's calling for me, rather than just something I wanted to do."*

Your business, my friend, is the perfect vehicle to go out into all the world with and share the love of Christ and His salvation and hope to those who'd never enter a church door, never sign up for a community Bible study and never read a tract left on their porch.

God has given you as a *light* to the Gentiles:
Thus saith God the Lord, he that created the heavens, and stretched them out; he that spread forth the earth, and that which cometh out of it; he that giveth breath unto the people upon it, and spirit to them that walk therein: I the Lord have called thee in righteousness, and will hold thine hand, and will keep thee, and give thee for a covenant of the people, for a light of the Gentiles; To open the blind eyes, to bring

out the prisoners from the prison, and them that sit in darkness out of the prison house. I am the Lord: that is my name: and my glory will I not give to another, neither my praise to graven images. Isaiah 42:5-8

You may be the only "Bible" influence those people ever have. You may be the only real Christian they ever interact with. I pray you will see just how great is the ministry to which you've been entrusted. May you be light for God's glory in your marketplace.

For Reflection:

My biggest takeaway from this chapter is....

The lie I have been believing is...

The truth I need to believe and act on is...

My action will be...

I will take this action on/by (date)...

14. Myth #6

BRINGING GOD INTO YOUR BUSINESS WILL YIELD FINANCIAL PROSPERITY

His lord said unto him, Well done, good and faithful servant; thou hast been faithful over a few things, I will make thee ruler over many things: enter thou into the joy of thy lord.
Matthew 25:23

I want to start off this chapter with a kind reminder to go back and reread chapter 6: Define Your Terms. It's imperative that you define success, prosperity and the goals of the business through the leading of the Holy Spirit in alignment with God's Word.

In light of the definitions of success and prosperity that you and The Owner decide are appropriate for the business in your hands, then go on to consider these truths...

The blessing of the Lord, it maketh rich, and he addeth no sorrow with it. Proverbs 10:22

But thou shalt remember the Lord thy God: for it is he that giveth thee power to get wealth, that he may establish his covenant which he sware unto thy fathers, as it is this day. Deuteronomy 8:18

Trust in the Lord, and do good; so shalt thou dwell in the land, and verily thou shalt be fed. Psalm 37:3

And why take ye thought for raiment? Consider the lilies of the field, how they grow; they toil not, neither do they spin: And yet I say unto you, That even Solomon in all his glory was not arrayed like one of these. Wherefore, if God so clothe the grass of the field, which to day is, and to morrow is cast into the oven, shall he not much more clothe you, O ye of little faith? Therefore take no thought, saying, What shall we eat? or, What shall we drink? or, Wherewithal shall we be clothed? (For after all these things do the Gentiles seek:) for your heavenly Father knoweth that ye have need of all these things. But seek ye first the kingdom of God, and his righteousness; and all these things shall be added unto you.
Matthew 6:28-33

God never promises lavish riches (outside of heaven). He does however promise to provide for us and to meet our needs. Although financial wealth comes from God, as do all good things (James 1:17), your primary goal in business is not to gain wealth for wealth's sake. Your objective is to steward well that which is entrusted to your care.

Jesus did not teach the pursuit of material, earthy riches. Because of this, it should not be your primary goal in business. Similarly, financial wealth and financial sacrifice or hardship should not be used to evaluate the power of one's faith or the extent of one's impact.

Wealth is a value humans attribute to an inanimate object here on earth. We get to choose to use it for good and Kingdom growth or for evil and selfish pleasure.

God has given sound principles in His Word by which you can manage money (and other assets of value) well and thus be considered capable to manage more. He has given principles which, when followed, will produce abundance. But here's the thing - His principles work even when followed by those who don't acknowledge Him as Creator or Savior. This is how there are many secular businesses run by non-believers on the top of the most successful business charts in our world today.

For he maketh his sun to rise on the evil and on the good, and sendeth rain on the just and on the unjust. Matthew 5:45

True prosperity that satisfies the soul is found in glorifying God.

When you seek to do that first and above all else, all of your needs will be met and then some.

I'll never forget the hot humid day I was sitting on the porch of our historic home in Mexico, hoping for a breeze to relieve the heat just a tad. I was having an inner discussion with God about our finances, well, really about what I saw as the lack of finances. I felt like we were doing all the right things in the business, a feeling affirmed by others. It just didn't feel like we could break the revenue slump we were in.

I was feeling pretty sorry for myself and a bit whiny. I mean, we'd been living in this house nearly 4 years and though we'd done a lot of work, we still hadn't been able to earn and save enough to install a proper kitchen. And for someone who's lived through 6 kitchen remodels in previous homes, I was really looking forward to enjoying this one sooner than I felt like it was happening. 4 years is a long time to prepare food for 7 on folding tables and garage shelving.

Then our 6 year old daughter came out and climbed up in my lap in the hammock chair, as she was prone to do whenever she found me there. She put her head on my shoulder and snuggled in breathing a huge contented sigh and asked, *"Mommy, are we rich?"*

Ouch! I had a choice. As I gulped and teared up, deciding how to respond, the wind picked up and the most amazing melody played through the wind chimes just above us. It was as if God was whispering to me, *"I haven't forgotten you. I'm here and I'm working to provide even though you don't always see it."*

Whispering a quick prayer of thanks, I pulled her closer and said,
"Oh yes! We're rich. God takes such good care of us. We have an amazing old house, food to eat, our kitty, and we're all healthy. We are very rich and very blessed."

Renewing my mind to the truth was key to changing my attitude, my perspective and my outlook which affected my impact on my very impressionable daughter. To this day she will tell you we are rich.

As you walk with God, learn to listen for His voice. Learn to master the principles and manage well what you have, then He can entrust you with more.

For unto every one that hath shall be given, and he shall have abundance: but from him that hath not shall be taken away even that which he hath. Matthew 25:29

He that is faithful in that which is least is faithful also in much: and he that is unjust in the least is unjust also in much. If therefore ye have not been faithful in the unrighteous mammon, who will commit to your trust the true riches? And if ye have not been faithful in that which is another man's, who shall give you that which is your own? No servant can serve two masters: for either he will hate the one, and love the other; or else he will hold to the one, and despise the other. Ye cannot serve God and mammon. Luke 16:10-13

And God blessed them, and God said unto them, Be fruitful, and multiply, and replenish the earth, and subdue it: and have dominion over the fish of the sea, and over the fowl of the air, and over every living thing that moveth upon the earth. Genesis 1:28

True prosperity can't be measured by a tax return. It is the prosperity of the soul that says *"It is well. God has supplied all I need. I am walking with Him today. I am doing what He's asked me to do today. I am mastering the care for the things He's entrusted to me today. And I am open to receiving more as He sends it and trusting Him to care for the rest."*

True prosperity can't be measured by a tax return.

One of my mastermind clients shared with me that according to her state, their family farm isn't profitable enough to even qualify for sales tax exemption and yet they are Kingdom focused and living their best lives. Here's what Dawnita[26] said: *"According to the IRS, even with 50 acres of land and a 100 year old two story home surrounded by livestock and pets, we live under "the poverty level." But we are living the life we've chosen. We have food in abundance and plenty of "things". There is no line between our ministry to the unchurched and our various businesses. When there is a need, God provides, either through additional work for our customers or through miracles we can share with others. As our children grow and move out, start families and businesses of their own, they are choosing similar paths, never even suggesting they want more than Kingdom living."*

For I have learned, in whatsoever state I am, therewith to be content.
Philippians 4:11

Before pursuing earthly possessions, your desire should be for God's blessing and His favor. Christian author Jeff Testerman says,[27] *"We need to pursue the blessing of blessing and favor of God in our lives so that we can become a conduit or a channel of God's blessing to the world around us."*

God's blessing in our business is not about us, friend. It's about God. It's about us being a channel for Him to bless people. When you see your abundance as something that is just administered for Him, when you see your business as a way to bless others, when you see money as a tool to do God's work with and when you see the income and the profit you make as a way for you to do more of God's work, then He can bless you with more. You have become a conduit, a channel of God's blessing, to the world around you. That's why you pursue His blessing and His favor in your business.

God wants to prosper us, but He also wants us to ask Him for what we need. Again, prosperity doesn't have to do with money or a bank account number. A prosperous soul is a soul that is mature in Christ. Sound in the wisdom of God, full of the love of God, full of love for God's people, full of love for the world. A prosperous soul is in daily fellowship with God and in His Word.

This book of the law shall not depart out of thy mouth; but thou shalt meditate therein day and night, that thou mayest observe to do according to all that is written therein: for then thou shalt make thy way prosperous, and then thou shalt have good success. Joshua 1:8

You can look up Joshua 1:8 on Biblegateway.com and see 51 different translations just in English. From what I could discover, the word translated *success* is mentioned in the Bible only in the Joshua 1:8 verse.
In 90% of the 51 translations of that verse, the word *success* has been translated as either *success* or *prosper*. *Prosper*, as in, to make you do well in all of these things. That is the only Scripture that uses that word *success*, and it's used in conjunction with *prosper*.

Before pursuing earthly possessions, your desire should be for God's blessing and His favor. Again Jeff Testerman says[28], *"When you have that prosperity of the soul, then you can handle any other kind of prosperity that God brings to you. Focus first on the prosperity of your soul."*

The other things will prosper as God wants them to. You focus first on prospering in maturity and love for God, and in your relationship with Him that brings peace and joy, and He will take care of the other things. When you have that maturity, then you can also be blessed with financial and material blessings that God wants to give you.

For Reflection:

My biggest takeaway from this chapter is....

The lie I have been believing is...

The truth I need to believe and act on is...

My action will be...

I will take this action
on/by (date)...

15. Myth #7

YOUR PEOPLE WILL COME FROM YOUR IMMEDIATE CIRCLES

No prophet is accepted in his own country.

Luke 4:24

When I was in college my friends and I would affectionately refer to our college campus as "the bubble". It was entirely possible to lead a lovely little existence within the bubble. Our campus included facilities for dining, lodging, recreation, education, laundry, special events, Sunday services, post office, shopping... you might say it was its own little world, but it wasn't the "real" world.

And yes, I know that for some it was in God's plan that they never leave. Some of my friends are still there, now as faculty or staff, serving the next generation, but most of us eventually left the bubble to put into practice what we'd learned and make our marks in the real world.

Not to burst your bubble, my friend, but the vast majority of believes have not been called to serve in a bubble. You're called to serve in the world, while also not being "of" the world.

Not to burst your bubble, my friend, but you're not called to serve in a bubble. You're called to serve in the world.

God says He sends us into the world because the world needs to know about Jesus.

And this gospel of the kingdom shall be preached in all the world for a witness unto all nations; and then shall the end come. Matthew 24:14

And he said unto them, Go ye into all the world, and preach the gospel to every creature. Mark 16:15

If all the world could be reached by each of us staying where we are and just sharing Jesus with the people we know now, there would have never been a need for the Great Commission.

Often I get shocked responses when I tell people that God is preparing their business to serve folks they don't even know yet. On the flip side, it's amazing how many are truly baffled and often hurt to discover their closest family members and friends aren't interested in supporting their business.

My friend and longtime client Danielle[29] always reminds me: *"The positive opinions of others are not a prerequisite for success."* meaning God is the one you have to please. He is in charge of bringing the people to me who need what He has prepared me to do for His glory, and I get to choose not to let the critique of those around have any bearing on the success of what He's doing in and through me.

I love the passage in Nehemiah where he answers those who were ploys of the enemy with intent to sabotage the work of rebuilding the ruins of Jerusalem's walls by criticizing them and their motives and essentially tells them they have no inheritance here and therefore no right to comment.

Then answered I them, and said unto them, The God of heaven, he will prosper us; therefore we his servants will arise and build: but ye have no portion, nor right, nor memorial, in Jerusalem. Nehemiah 2:20

In Matthew 13:57 Jesus said, *"A prophet is not without honour, save in his own country, and in his own house."*

And just before leaving earth He told the disciples: *"Ye shall be witnesses unto me both in Jerusalem, and in all Judaea, and in Samaria, and unto the uttermost part of the earth".* Acts 1:8

There are two ways to understand and apply His words: literally or figuratively.
In the literal interpretation, you apply Jesus' words in a physical sense, in terms of distance. It is a charge to share the Gospel with the city of Jerusalem (where they already were), and for you to share the Gospel with your city, which includes your neighbors and your local community.

Next, to expand to the close by region of Judea, the people in the wider region where you live, the country you are a citizen of. And then, there is a global perspective, the charge to go to the geographically further away and culturally different region of Samaria, or in other words, other nations of the world. And finally to all the ends of the earth.

Acts 1:8 can also be interpreted in a more symbolic way. Considering the various levels of intimacy you have with other people, the charge to share the Gospel could be applied to different relationships in your life beginning with your immediate family or close friends. Then move on to your sphere of influence outside of your closest circle and finally to those who are culturally and/or socially different from you.

And there is no better vehicle than business (in my opinion) to take you to those acquaintances and those culturally and socially different from you, who need not just your services, but your Jesus.

The great author C.S. Lewis[30] believed he could use the business of writing and book publishing for the "re-conversion" of the entire nation of England. He desired to see the best work on the market authored by a Christian regardless of topic or area of study. He wanted to see believers influencing people for Christ from the tops of their fields, not just in religious arenas, but in all niches carrying out the "yeast work" that Jesus spoke of in Matthew.

The kingdom of heaven is like unto leaven, which a woman took, and hid in three measures of meal, till the whole was leavened. Matthew 13:33.

Don't expect all of your current connections to understand, approve of or participate with your business. You may or may not be the one God's designed to help them take their next step. But also don't be discouraged if they're not interested. God didn't give you this business for nothing. He knows who needs you and even now is preparing you for each other as He brings them to you.

Your Father knoweth what things ye have need of, before ye ask him. Matthew 6:8

Trust Him.

For Reflection:

My biggest takeaway from this chapter is....

The lie I have been believing is...

The truth I need to believe and act on is...

My action will be...

I will take this action on/by (date)...

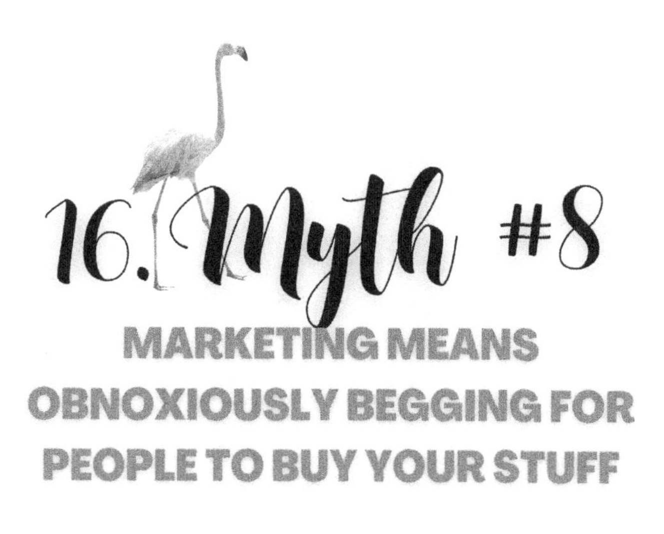

16. Myth #8

MARKETING MEANS OBNOXIOUSLY BEGGING FOR PEOPLE TO BUY YOUR STUFF

But my God shall supply all your need according to
his riches in glory by Christ Jesus.
Philippians 4:19

"*Tell me what you think of when you hear the word "marketing"*. I asked this of a couple hundred people at one of our marketing masterclasses[31]. Here are some of the responses they turned in:

- Promoting yourself as top in your niche.
- Convincing people to buy.
- Bragging about stuff and sharing opportunities.
- Making people aware of your products/service and the benefits they offer.
- Using different means to bring awareness to others about your product or services including advertising, discounts or offers to incentivize them to act upon a desire to use or try your service.
- Irritating people with boring sales pitches.
- Ads, shameless plugs, newsletter swaps, work, work, work...

Their answers were charged with negative and emotional words. This shows how greatly a couple of generations and cultural changes can influence our understanding of everyday words.

The Merriam-Webster 1828 Dictionary gives this definition of the verb:

market: *verb*, To deal in market; to buy or sell; to make bargains for provisions or goods.

Interestingly enough, the word *marketing* didn't even make it into the 1828 resource. The current online dictionary defines it this way:

marketing: *noun*, the act or process of selling or purchasing in a market, OR the process or technique of promoting, selling, and distributing a product or service. 2. The activities involved in moving goods from producer to consumer.[32]

The stark difference between what the word is said to mean and what the people I spoke to understood it to mean lies in the emotions of the word. People have attached a negative emotion to the process of what otherwise should be a normal, healthy, even valuable everyday activity for all involved.

What happened? How did we get here? I believe we've lost ourselves in the lie that your business is for you. We have forgotten that business is about what God wants to do for others through the abilities He's entrusted to you.

Business is about what God wants to do for others through the abilities He's entrusted to you.

In creating a business marketing strategy, the goal is generally to grow your reach and provide your opportunity to more people, so that a greater number of people will buy from you and receive the transformation you provide.

This is where it is extremely important to be clear on God's goals for the business. In the big picture of things, what is the end goal? And how can you get there?

I think it's important to point out too that not all marketing is "paid marketing." The process of promoting, selling and fulfilling on sales is greatly enhanced or inhibited by the reputation of the company even in the moments and activities that are not specifically marketing related.

If you're the CEO of a secular company and you are bad-mouthing the owner, you will not be CEO for long.

We all understand that, and yet it seems we think we can get away with complaining and whining about our business and lot in life with no recompense.

Complaining comes from a heart that says, *"I really don't believe God is in control of this. I really don't believe God has my best interest at heart. I really don't believe God made the best choice here."*

So you see how complaining puts you above God. That's bad-mouthing the CEO. That's saying you know better than God.

Philippians 2:14 says, *"Do all things without murmurings and disputings."*

This is a bigger command than you may first realize. It doesn't just affect your personal life, but your professional life and business results as well.

What about begging? Begging in Bible days was a sign of the outcast. The outcast was the one who sat and begged, asking for alms or donations for himself. And this is why looking back, I believe it was so difficult for us as traditional independent missionaries to raise our own funding. I couldn't put my finger on it back then, but now I believe that what we felt and struggled with was the incongruence of what we were told we needed to do vs. Scriptural principles... and that's likely best left as a topic for another book.

Have you seen business owners post things like this on social media? *"Please buy from me. My family has had such a hard time. I just need a couple of sales. This is so hard for me. I don't know why it's not working. Why don't people buy from me, please, please, please, please, please..."*

Does that give God a good name? Are you believing in your heart that God is your all good, all-powerful, all-sovereign provider when you're begging? What picture of God are you showing the world when you're begging for your next dollar?

When you beg or complain about lack, and even when you try in your own strength to "sell" your products and services without truly believing that God is your provider and is responsible for and capable of providing your needs, you're out of alignment.

In her book *Switch on Your Brain,*[33] Dr. Caroline Leaf says: *"You can't imagine and feel, change your brain structurally one way, and speak something different; because if you do there will be a lack of integrity operating in your brain which will leave an overwhelming feeling of being out of control."*

This is why the secular practice of "pitching" or "selling someone" feels so icky to a believer. You need to go back to Scripture and learn who God is and let that instruct your sales process and the words you use to refer to it.

God is your provider. God is faithful. God owns it all. He does not need you to ask anyone but Him for provision. You have no need to be sitting on the sidelines, begging for people to meet your needs when your Father owns everything and has put a business in your hands that can meet your needs. You need to be going to Him to find out where that provision will come from, and then going to people not to sell so you can gain, but to sell so they can receive the blessing of transformation in their life.

Be not ye therefore like unto them: for your Father knoweth what things ye have need of, before ye ask him. Matthew 6:8

God knows what you need before you ask. He's already providing for you. He's already in tomorrow, preparing to fulfill that need.

Even in the beginning, when Tap and I had just five dollars in the bank, even when we didn't know where the next meal was coming from, even when we didn't know if we'd have enough money coming in to pay our power bill for the next month, never once did God forsake us. Never once did we go hungry. Never once did we not have enough.

God always provides for what He calls you to do. Just as in the story of the Prodigal son (Luke 15:11-32), you and I have no need to be out there giving God a bad name by begging when we could be talking to our Father who owns it all.

Complaining verbally or publicly on social media is not giving God a good name in front of the people that you're trying to reach either. I'm not saying to be fake. It's okay to be authentic enough to admit you have bad days. You are human after all. But if everything you do should be done to the glory of God (1 Corinthians 10:31) then you've got to find a way to refrain from the complaint and say something that gives Him glory or it is best left unsaid.

A CEO does not complain, whine, grovel or beg people to invest in your company. You're proud of your company and what it can do for your clients and customers. You have confidence in The Owner. You have confidence in the power of the product or service. You know the good it will do and the transformation it will bring to their lives. You're proud of that in a good way and that gives confidence.

Another quality of a good CEO of marketing is that you don't demand your rights. The CEO is always looking out for the good of the company.

What shall we say then? Shall we continue in sin, that grace may abound? God forbid. How shall we, that are dead to sin, live any longer therein?...For he that is dead is freed from sin. Romans 6:1-2, 7

If you look at Romans chapter six, it's all about being dead to sin and alive to Christ. So if you have died to the old man, you have died to sin. You have no rights.

A dead man has no rights.

For I through the law am dead to the law, that I might live unto God. I am crucified with Christ: nevertheless I live; yet not I, but Christ liveth in me: and the life which I now live in the flesh I live by the faith of the Son of God, who loved me, and gave himself for me. Galatians 2:19-20

You have no rights to something that makes you look good. It's all about Him now. He's made you new in Him. This is about God. It's all about Him.

You have no right to be obnoxious.
You have no right to offend.
You have no right to be cheesy or annoying.
You have no right to use language, illustrations or marketing strategies that are in contradiction to God's standards or less than glorifying to Him.

The flesh that had those rights is a dead man and those rights expired with him.

The business God has given you is a tool with which to bring Him glory.

I'll never forget being at a secular business event where the guest speaker was someone who has a growing following and an established name as a teacher of Christians in his niche. At this particular event many of the speakers made references to drinking in their talks. And as he was setting up to make a particular point in his presentation, this Christian speaker also chose to use the illustration of a person walking into a bar and ordering a cocktail... The story was appropriate to the audience and the atmosphere, but totally inappropriate to the reputation he'd built as a Christian leader and the opportunity in front of him.

My heart twisted inside and my eyes teared up as it hit me that he'd just chosen to identify with the world with a few insignificant details. The location and menu choice details had no bearing on the marketing point he was making. He could just as easily have said he'd walked into a restaurant and ordered coffee or french fries and it would not have damaged his reputation or detracted from his point.

I grieved to see that someone claiming the name of Christ had been handed a platform and an opportunity to shine God's glory and instead of even choosing to remain neutral, he'd tried to appear "just like them".

During the break after the session, a couple of people asked me *"but isn't he a Christian?"* Another friend overhearing said *"I didn't know him before today, and from his talk I wouldn't have guessed he was a believer if I hadn't heard your conversation."*

And please, don't make the mistake of making this about drinking and miss the point I'm trying to make here. Whether drinking is or isn't ok for believers is a discussion for another day. The point is that a simple choice of words could have maintained his testimony for the Lord in front of a larger audience. Choosing instead to identify with the world damaged his influence with those who did know what he stands for, and also greatly diminished his chances of attracting more Christians from that event to his business. He lost his testimony and forfeited a huge opportunity.

The business God has given you is a tool with which to bring Him glory. Your position and opportunities are only because of Him, and it's all about Him and what He can do in this world through you, not the other way around. When you can get clear on this point, your marketing will feel easy and enjoyable.

When your focus is on what God is doing in the world through the business and on how God wants to help others through you and you're excited about it, it won't be nearly as hard. You won't need to hide it or be offensive or annoying about it because the people on the receiving end will feel His love.

And if they don't - because there are always a few who just choose to be offended regardless - you also have no right to be offended by those who would take offense and come against you for honoring God with your business or marketing.

I am crucified with Christ: nevertheless I live; yet not I, but Christ liveth in me: and the life which I now live in the flesh I live by the faith of the Son of God, who loved me, and gave himself for me. Galatians 2:20

Great peace have they which love thy law: and nothing shall offend them. Psalm 119:165

You get to do everything you can to build bridges and create relationships, not tear them down. You have opportunities to share the love and the light of Christ with these people that He has called you to serve. Whether or not they accept your invitation is totally between them and the Lord. It's He who brings in the results.

So then neither is he that planteth any thing, neither he that watereth; but God that giveth the increase. 1 Corinthians 3:7

For Reflection:

My biggest takeaway from this chapter is....

The lie I have been believing is...

The truth I need to believe and act on is...

My action will be...

I will take this action on/by (date)...

'IF YOU'RE STILL BREATHING, THERE IS STILL A JOB FOR YOU TO DO AND A PURPOSE FOR YOUR LIFE.'

KATIE HORNOR

PART THREE

Change THE WORLD

A 7-PART FRAMEWORK FOR LEGACY CHANGE

17. Makeover YOUR MINDSET

And be not conformed to this world: but be ye transformed by the renewing of your mind, that ye may prove what is that good, and acceptable, and perfect, will of God.

Romans 12:2

In the movie *The Incredibles*[34], there's a little guy who invents his own flying boots and cape so he can be like the "super heroes". He says, *"When everybody's super, no one will be!"* He's looking for acceptance, belonging, significance. But in trying to become like those he admired he overlooked his own unique abilities.

You and I are often like this. We believe if we all had the same talents and gifts as others we'd be better off. The reality is, there would be nothing interesting in the world. The world would be a boring place if we were all the same. It's our differences, the uniqueness of who God has created us to be, that makes life interesting.

That uniqueness also makes marketing interesting as each of us participate in a small way in God's big plan to glorify Himself in the world. There are lots of people who may be able to do what you do. That's great market validation. It's a good thing. And there is *no one* in the world who does what you do exactly like *you* do it. And that is what I call your unique flamingo advantage.

You can reach people that I will never be able to reach. My children will reach people that I will never be able to reach. Some of us may overlap. There are other people who teach business from a biblical perspective. I'm not the only one. Even though much of our audiences may travel in both circles, they will reach some people I won't and I'll reach some people they won't. It's not a threat. It's a blessing. We're not competitors. It means we get to work together to better serve a greater number of people!

You have a specific message that God has gifted you, put in your heart and needs to go out. No matter what the actual business is, no matter what the channel is, you're glorifying God by getting that message out. Your ability to change the world through your business and the message you carry is not as much about what you do as about who you serve. You've been called to display His glory and open their eyes to see Him.

I the Lord have called thee in righteousness, and will hold thine hand, and will keep thee, and give thee for a covenant of the people, for a light of the Gentiles; To open the blind eyes, to bring out the prisoners from the prison, and them that sit in darkness out of the prison house. Isaiah 42:6-8

Even if your business isn't explicitly a Christian business, even if you're not using religious catchphrases in your marketing, there is a way for you to let the Holy Spirit work in you and through you for God's glory and to accomplish His purposes on earth, but you must choose to believe it.

I often hear Christian entrepreneurs saying *"I'm not enough. I'm not good enough to do this. I don't know enough. I don't have enough experience, etc..."* The world would have you believe and repeat the empty affirmation "I am enough" fifteen times, kiss your reflection in the mirror three times, high five your dog, put on your big girl pants, drop your lucky penny in your pocket and keep going.

I will just tell you straight out - you're right. You're not enough.

You're not enough.
But there's a remedy for that
and His name is Jesus.

The truth you need to believe, meditate and act upon is that God is enough. God *is* enough! If God has called you to this, this is not about you. It's about Him.

If He has called you to this, He has already promised to do through you what He's called you to do. You don't need to be enough. You need to makeover your mindset and base your beliefs on truth.

Faithful is he that calls you who also will do it. 1 Thessalonians 5:24

Faithful is He who calls you. That doesn't mean you have to do it in your own strength. It means God is promising to do it through you if He's called you to this. Jesus didn't call and train preachers and priests to change the world with His message; He called everyday tradespeople.

He wants you to be the one out there in His marketplace. You're the one interacting with people every day in everyday situations, in everyday stresses, with everyday questions, and everyday worries. He wants you to give them hope and help. To show them how their lives can change through what He can do through you. It's His ministry, and He's called you to this so that He can work through you what He wants to do in their lives.

You are not enough, my friend, but God is. And He's already promised to do the work He's called you to.

God is faithful. There's never been a moment in our life when He did not provide. I couldn't see it sometimes, but that didn't mean He wasn't providing. I didn't know what the next step was sometimes, but that didn't mean He wasn't already there. I didn't know how growing our business was going to happen, but that didn't mean it wasn't going to happen.

He does the calling. He does the work. He just wants you and I to be willing.

Somebody once said it takes several years to become an overnight success story. A lot of times, that's the way we feel about business and success.

And again, this is not a prosperity gospel. This is not a magic pill. We're not talking about Jack and the Magic Beanstalk beans here. This is a daily choice to walk with God, to learn of God, to do what He asks you to do. That is success on a daily basis and it comes by renewing your mind.

There is no magic pill.
It's a daily choice to walk with God
and renew your mind.

You've got to replace the false beliefs you have been holding to so tightly all of your life with truth. And to replace them with truth, you've got to know the Truth. This is why God tells us to meditate in His Words day and night:

Blessed is the man that walketh not in the counsel of the ungodly, nor standeth in the way of sinners, nor sitteth in the seat of the scornful. But his delight is in the law of the Lord; and in his law doth he meditate day and night. And he shall be like a tree planted by the rivers of water, that bringeth forth his fruit in his season; his leaf also shall not wither; and whatsoever he doeth shall prosper. Psalm 1:1-3

This book of the law shall not depart out of thy mouth; but thou shalt meditate therein day and night, that thou mayest observe to do according to all that is written therein: for then thou shalt make thy way prosperous, and then thou shalt have good success. Joshua 1:8

Learn to immerse yourself in truth because what comes from the heart goes to the head. As you think on the truth, it begins to come out in your words and actions. You must know Truth to believe truth to think on truth and act on it consistently. It takes practice.

Doing business *with* God allows you to experience ultimately being at peace with Him, being at peace with yourself, your family, and with your business. Because now you have true beliefs as the basis allowing you to clearly think on truth in every situation, business or not. Then you'll have the energy and the passion to go where God is leading you.

When you're clear on what God wants you to do and why He wants you to do it, there is excitement, not dread.

When you listen for God, and when God directs you, you're able to make decisions that allow your dreams to come true.

I asked some of my coaching clients what their perfect day would look like if a miracle happened and everything was the way they wished it would be. Not one mentioned a dollar number.

Several mentioned peace or confidence. Several said things like having more time with family or ministry.... The thing is, you don't have to wait for your business to generate millions to have those things. You can have them now. Those are the kinds of things that you can have today when you walk with the Lord, applying His principles to your work, time and resources.

When you listen to Him daily, you know you can keep your thoughts in the right place no matter what's thrown at you. You can know beyond any doubt that you are successful in every area of your life through Jesus Christ. All of this comes back to knowing God.

Think about the difference between a real life flamingo and one of those pink flamingo inner tubes, the kind you blow up and float around in your pool. They're both pink. They're both flamingos. They both float on water.

A pink flamingo floatie will not go far. You're going to have to go back and re-inflate every so often. The sun hitting that plastic of the inner tube makes air escape little by little, and pretty soon it's going to deflate and it will not float anymore. There is no protection from an alligator for a pink flamingo inner tube on the river. He'll be lunch in no time. His place is in a calm pool under a shaded, screened porch somewhere.

Put a real flamingo in that same "safe" environment and he'll die for lack of food and lack space. He needs to be where he can travel where he wills, float to his heart's content, and even though danger exists in his habitat, he's equipped to use his wings and fly away when it approaches. He can find his own food and impact change in a global ecosystem because that's what God created him for.

In your own strength, you can do some things that you need to do to make your businesses successful. That's the way natural law works. If you blow up a pink flamingo inner tube, it will float–for a while. But it can't sustain life on the water or fly, because only the flamingos that God gives life to do that.

When I think about doing what God designed me to do, I don't want to be a pink flamingo inner tube. I don't even want to be a flamingo in captivity. I want to be a real flamingo, fulfilling my purpose in the space God created me for.

Be a flamingo.

Not an inner tube.

But let him that glorieth glory in this, that he understandeth and knoweth me, that I am the Lord which exercise lovingkindness, judgment, and righteousness, in the earth: for in these things I delight, saith the Lord. Jeremiah. 9:24

But the salvation of the righteous is of the Lord: he is their strength in the time of trouble. Psalm 37:39

All of our glory, strength and reward comes from knowing Christ. That's where the blessings are. That's when we get to see all the exciting things God is doing in our lives and businesses.

Grace and peace be multiplied unto you through the knowledge of God, and of Jesus our Lord. 2 Peter 1:2

How do you get peace? By knowing God. And why does that give you peace? Because when you know God, you know Him as all powerful and in control. If He's all powerful and He's in control, then do you have anything to fear? Is there anything to be anxious about if God's got this? No, there's not! That gives peace, because you know God, and you know who He is. There's also the peace that comes from loving God's word.

Great peace have they which love thy law: and nothing shall offend them.
Psalm 119:165

How do you have the peace that keeps you from getting all worked up and tied in internal knots when somebody criticizes, questions or says something about you? You love His law, staying peaceful in your soul and knowing God.

Loving God's law produces peace.
Peace produces confidence.

When you are confident, that means nothing shakes you. Nothing upsets your apple cart. Nothing rocks your boat when you are confident. You can be confident in what He's asked you to do, confident in where you're going with this business and confident in His direction.

You will not be moved, because you have confidence in the One who's called you to this and who's directing the business. Confidence comes from knowing God, and trusting in Him based on His previous workings.

If you'd like to learn more about faith working itself out in daily life, go read Hebrews chapter eleven. Remind yourself what God has done throughout the centuries of history. We get confidence in part by rehearsing the great works of God in the past to ourselves and to others.

This gives confidence because it helps you know Him better. It's easier to believe His promises to you when you read the testimonies of His work in others' lives.

He is today who He has always been. He is faithful. He does not change. So, if He did that in the past, He can do that for you today. It gives confidence because you know Him, because you trust Him to be who He said He would be. You trust Him to keep His word and to keep His promises. You trust His choice. Again, being confident in God and His investment in choosing you to do this.

Sometimes I wake up and I'm just amazed. How cool is it that I get to do this? It's so awesome! God chose me. He created me. He gave me all the life experiences and all the training I needed to do this thing that I'm doing right now helping Christian coaches and course businesses grow their income and legacy impact in the Kingdom and shine God's glory to the world. And that is so thrilling. Knowing that gives me confidence.

The other thing that gives you confidence is surrounding yourself with people who will speak life into you.

Those who walk with wise men shall be wise. Proverbs 13:20

You will be confident as you surround yourself with those who speak life into you not those who speak criticism, and not those who speak negatively or out of fear. You need to choose specifically, on purpose, to be with the people who will build you up in Christ.

Community is one of the main core values in our business. It's a big part of why our main offerings are no longer do it yourself courses but mastermind groups and course experiences with communities and coaching built in.[35] You and I were not meant to do life or business alone. We need face to face relationships for both joy and change.

For true transformation and lasting change you need to surround yourself not only with those who can encourage you but with those who share your values and beliefs and are willing to challenge and correct your false beliefs with the truth, giving and receiving godly wisdom from one another. If you don't have that, begin seeking it today. If not in one of our programs, find one somewhere where you can get the edification and support you need as you do His most important work.

All scripture is given by inspiration of God, and is profitable for doctrine, for reproof, for correction, for instruction in righteousness: That the man of God may be perfect, thoroughly furnished unto all good works. 2 Timothy 3:16-17

And again - this is not just about you and finding a group who can support you and build you up, but you also need to choose specifically to be one of those people who gives it out, who builds others up in Christ. You may have seen a quote talking about being the girl who fixes another's crown. Don't just fix her crown, fix her hair, fix her skirt. Don't just shout all the tips, help her out. That's who you need to be and who you can more easily become when you are surrounded by others who are like minded in the faith.

The formula for confidence is knowing God, knowing what He's done for others and through others, knowing who He is and that He keeps His promises. He's the same tomorrow as He was yesterday. If He did it before, He can do it again.

This is the reason to use testimonials and endorsements in your marketing too, by the way. It's often easier for people to take another person's word that something worked than the creator's word. It's easier for you to see yourself in another person's story than in the facts and statistics. It's easier to believe it for yourself when you hear it testified by another.

There is also grace and glory in knowing God and resetting your mind to His truth.

Grace and peace be multiplied unto you through the knowledge of God, and of Jesus our Lord. 2 Peter 1:2

Do you know what grace is? There are two definitions of grace. If you look up the word, one definition is divine enablement. God may give you grace to do or withstand something. He may give you His enablement to do something you couldn't have done on your own.
The other definition of grace is unmerited or undeserved favor. Favor is reward. All of us have way more in life than we deserve. And the wonderful thing is, God desires to give us even more.

In the same way that you enjoy spoiling the loved ones in your life, God enjoys doing special things for those of us who can manage those blessings in a way that brings Him glory. That is His favor.

And according to 2 Peter 1:2 you receive His favor when you know Him. It says through the knowledge of God, this grace will be multiplied to you. Here's another verse with the same promise:

For the Lord God is a sun and shield: the Lord will give grace and glory: no good thing will he withhold from them that walk uprightly. Psalm 84:11

There's that word again: grace and glory. No good thing will He withhold from them that walk uprightly.

Do you think God doesn't care about things? He just said *"no good thing will I withhold from you, if you walk uprightly."*

So then you have to ask, *"What does walking uprightly mean?"* It means walking with Him and walking in righteousness.

Let's look at the first part of that verse, *"the Lord God is a sun and the shield."*

What does the sun do? It provides light, vitamin D, growth. Additionally, it provides nutrients to plants and the plants produce oxygen, which helps us breathe. They also feed us, giving us provision.

What is a shield? A shield provides protection and proclaims our identity in the Kingdom. In the olden days, when they would hold up their shields in battle, all the shields had emblems on them showing or "heralding" to the enemy whose side they were on. So a shield is not just protection, a shield is also identification. It shows who you are and whose side you're on.

God is your sun and your shield. Do your marketing and business policies show your identity as heir of His Kingdom? as an ambassador or officer of the King?

It also says He will "give grace." He will give that undeserved favor and He will "give glory."

What is glory? In this case, it's recognition or honor. It is a reward to those who walk uprightly.

Know therefore that the Lord thy God, he is God, the faithful God, which keepeth covenant and mercy with them that love him and keep his commandments to a thousand generations. Deuteronomy 7:9

But my God shall supply all your need according to his riches in glory by Christ Jesus. Philippians 4:19

God keeps His covenant to us for generations. He promises to supply all of your needs. This is the reward of being His child, it is the reward of your position in Him, in His Kingdom and most assuredly in His business.

Peace, confidence, and reward in life and in business all come when you believe God's truths about Himself and His Word and yourself and you renew your mind constantly toward those beliefs.

For Reflection:

My biggest takeaway from this chapter is....

The truth I need to believe and act on is...

My action will be...

I will take this action on/by (date)...

18. Align YOUR VISION

Where there is no vision, the people perish:
but he that keepeth the law, happy is he.
Proverbs 29:18

When God calls you to business, it is a spiritual thing. Doing what God has called you to do is just as spiritual as if you were called into full-time ministry.

If that's been a new thought for you as you've read this book, I want to invite you to think about what our Lord says in the New Testament concerning how each of us receives different gifts:

Having then gifts differing according to the grace that is given to us...
Romans 12:6

His favor and enablement is given differently to different people. Those gifts in a business setting may take the form of administration, apostleship, compassion, connection, creativity, cross-cultural ministry/

business, discernment, encouragement, evangelism, faith, giving, hospitality, intercessory prayer, knowledge, leadership, pastoring, prophecy, service, teaching, wisdom, and more.

All of those gifts work together in the body for the benefit of everyone, for all the believers in the church of Christ.

When you are doing the business that God has called you to do, living for Him as you do that business, focused on serving and glorifying Him by using your spiritual gifting, and giving your excellence by doing your best, loving the people He brings to you through your business–that is worship. That is a spiritual job, because that is what He's called you to do.

There's nothing more spiritual than doing what God has asked you to do. We're not toys, but to put this in the context of a very simple example: nothing honors the toymaker more than a toy that does what it was created to do. Doing otherwise would mean the toymaker made a mistake. God does not make mistakes. You and your gifts and abilities are not a mistake.

There's nothing more obedient than doing what God asked you to do. Nothing can bring Him more honor than doing what you were created to do. Don't let anyone tell you that you cannot be a Christian in the workplace. Don't let anyone tell you that you cannot blend your faith with your career. Don't let anyone tell you that you can't honor God in your marketing because doing what God has called you to do is your best worship - even if the location you do it in is a secular field.

Following Him in your business is walking in faith. It is your service of love to Him to do what He's called to do. If you do it with His glory in mind and with His love in your heart for those people you are engaging with during the course of that work, that is worship and walking in faith.

My mentor Jeff Walker[36] once said: *"It is your sacred duty to serve the world in this way and to over deliver because this is the gift you've been given to give the world, regardless of whether they buy your course at the end of launch or not."*

For a Christian, your business is ministry. This is the gift you have been appointed to give the world, not simply to generate revenue with it - but to change the world with it! Let God take care of the revenue.

Have you been believing the lie that you cannot worship God through business, or that a secular career is somehow less than a full-time ministry career? I'll say it again because it's that important:

Doing what God has called you to do,
***is* your best worship.**

It is a spiritual assignment and you can do it with the goal of glorifying Him and doing your absolute best to serve Him through everything that you do in this business. You can take every opportunity to show Christ to the people in your marketplace.

True believers don't separate who you are from what you do in business. You don't separate your faith and your business, your values and your business, your family and your business. You blend them. You align them all to match with the goals of the One who's called you to this.

A flamingo doesn't pretend not to be a flamingo when he's feeding and then go back to being a flamingo when he's flying. That's silly. And yet some Christians think it makes perfect sense to "do church" and "be spiritual" on Sundays, then go live like the world, conduct business like the world and run marketing campaigns like the world the rest of the week, because they think they cannot mix faith and business.

As a believer in business, you must bring all of yourself everywhere you are and be fully present in that moment, responsive to the Holy Spirit's leading in whatever activity the moment calls for.

Ask yourself *"What does it look like for me to live in alignment with who God is and who I am authentically, in every sphere of my life?"*

It is important to be aware and accepting of the fact that things die. Death precedes life; a seed buried in the ground has to die before it can bring forth life. Sometimes you have a great idea in your head and you're all gung ho and yet the Holy Spirit shuts that door. You must be willing to say, *"Okay Lord, what is it You want? What do You want me to do? Help me hold my ideas loosely until I have the confirmation that they are also your ideas and your will for me."* Then as He gives confirmation you can follow them gung ho as the Lord brings His plans for you to life.

I once applied for a higher level secular business mastermind with a group of business owners I already know and am fond of. Due to the circumstances around learning of the opening, I was excited and convinced it was God's next step for our business. So when they declined my application after months of waiting, it was a bit of a shock. Tap and I trusted that God was opening and closing doors according to His purposes though and began asking "*What other opportunity does God want us to see?*"

Within days of getting that news I was invited to apply to Dan Miller's *EaglePreneurs Mastermind*[37] where I was promptly admitted and welcomed by a group of entirely new to me Christian business owners with similar values and varied gifts, experiences, and connections.

Every meeting has provided something I've been able to tweak in our business or marketing to improve ourselves and our service. As it turns out the mastermind was indeed God's next step for us, though not the one I'd initially set my sights on. I can't imagine what blessings we might have missed had I not followed His prompting to apply for the first opportunity and thus been open and looking for the second.

Don't hold on to anything so tightly that it throws you out of alignment with God's purposes because what He wants for you is always better than any imagined ideas you can come up with on your own.

Delight thyself also in the Lord: and he shall give thee the desires of thine heart.
Psalm 37:4

I think often we misrepresent Psalm 37:4. If you want a better handle on it, read verses 1-9 of the passage. Verse 4 is not saying to put God first and then you can do whatever you want. It's saying, if you are seeking God first, if you are delighting yourself in Him, then He is able to awaken in you the desires that He placed in you and wants you to have, which are going to be desires He can happily fulfill.

When you are trusting in God, already doing "good things" in His name, committing your way to Him, looking for Him to prosper your work, resting in Him, He will not let you miss those desires He's placed in you. He's not going to let you make a bad decision if your true heart's desire is to serve Him. He's going to put those desires in your heart, which are things He wants to fulfill. It's almost as if He's saying, *"I'm going to place in her a desire for this, because I want to see her delight when she receives (or achieves) it."* Does that make sense?

God puts those desires in you that He wants you to have so He can give you the desires of your heart. He actually plants desires in your heart and then He can fulfill them for (or through) you. What an amazing truth!

So often I see students or clients struggling to take action because they are "waiting on God" to reveal which action to take.

My friend, if God has given you the vision and good options are in front of you, make a choice and take action! In Deuteronomy 15:16 and 24:19 God says He'll bless the work of your hands. That blessing presupposes your hands are working, not sitting around waiting!

If you have the vision and good options in front of you, make a choice and take action! The blessing presupposes your hands are working, not sitting around waiting!

When faced with a decision, if your options are good and good, I believe you are free to choose the one you desire because they're both good decisions. God allows us that free will to choose and make those decisions. If God is pleased with both option A and option B, then you have only to decide which one do you want to do?

If God doesn't want you there, I believe He'll shut the door. He's going to make it obvious that's not where you're supposed to go. But if not, then you're at complete liberty to choose whichever one of those good options He has placed before you.

Yes, you can seek wise counsel, and balance it with knowing that no one else knows what God is speaking to your heart. No one else has been given your vision. It's yours. You don't need another human's permission or approval to obey what God asks you to do, but you must take action in alignment with His Word and with the vision and desire He's given.

For Reflection:

My biggest takeaway from this chapter is....

The truth I need to believe and act on is...

My action will be...

I will take this action on/by (date)...

19. Refine YOUR EXPECTATIONS

Wealth gotten by vanity shall be diminished: but he that gathereth by labour shall increase. Hope deferred maketh the heart sick: but when the desire cometh, it is a tree of life.

Proverbs 13:11-12

It's 8:30am and my phone is flashing a message. I pick it up and smile as I hit the off button. The alarm message reads: *"Be grateful. You used to pray for days like this. God is doing good things today."* And I am grateful. I have indeed prayed for days like this, and God has given abundantly more than I deserve. He has never ceased to be good in the midst of even the darkest hours He has walked us through.

God honors the natural laws of the world He created. It is possible for one to do good work and get great results with little to no knowledge of God. To return to the farmer example, you can study everything about having a successful farm business. You can have a good crop, and you can make a good profit. But when you study everything humanly possible and you yield the results to the God of the harvest to bless that crop, your results can be even more.

The farmer counts the cost of the sowing, weighs the risk and potential gain. He then sows the seed expecting a multiplication in the harvest. He cares for the seed as it grows and multiplies, protecting his investment until it matures.

In your line of work, whatever that may be, you want to do everything humanly possible to be excellent in all that you do so you can get the results you expect for your effort. You can also choose to yield the results to God, who knows all and is all powerful and sovereign over those results. As you do, ask Him for His creative ideas to do your work well, for multiplication and blessing. Be ready to praise Him and honor Him as He works in your life and business.

As you think about your expectations, also think about your long term goals. You don't create marketing funnels, make sales calls and run email campaigns in your business just for a quick cash infusion today and tomorrow we'll figure out tomorrow... or at least you shouldn't be operating that way. There should be a long-term goal in mind, a set of actions planned to get there and an expected return on the investment.

What are you working for? What desires has God put in your heart for the future? Do you have a people impact goal, a revenue generation goal, something else you want to achieve? Why does what you do matter? And what results are you expecting?

God gave this vision to you. No one else is going to make it happen if you don't.

In 2018, my husband Tap and I had a vision. A dream to impact people all around the world and teach them to do business *with* God and multiply their impact. We had a desire to teach them to get their message to the world with integrity and love, while at the same time allowing us to be fully present with our kids and fully able to embrace any opportunity for speaking or ministry that might arise.

We also had a dream that our business would fund the restoration of our historic home so that someday we would be able to offer a safe place of healing for hurting ministry families and a welcoming hope to travelers in search of truth.

We decided we wanted that dream to look like:

1. Morning quiet time and coffee and evening conversations in the hammock chairs on our hacienda porch.
2. Conducting business activities 3-4 days a week, doing more of what we loved, but working fewer hours and enjoying it instead of always looking forward to the next vacation from work.
3. Regularly speaking to inspire, challenge and equip others with the knowledge and skills we've been given.
4. Plenty enough income to provide for our family and ministry opportunities the Lord would bring.

5. Regular activities and outings with our kids while they're still young enough for us to actively influence their learning and world view for Christ.
6. Prioritizing house restoration projects one at a time.
7. Making time for hobbies and bucket list items.
8. Saying yes more.

Now it's your turn. Describe your dream day. What does your dream day look like in your life and in your business? Take a moment to make some notes guided by the following questions:

- Where do you live?
- In what kind of home?
- How do you wake up?
- What's your morning routine look like?
- What do you do?
- Do you spend time with family?
- Do you spend time doing work activities?
- Do you spend time with clients?
- Is fitness part of your daily life?
- What about hobbies?
- Are you traveling?
- Are you in the community?
- Are you doing ministry work?
- What kinds of impact are you having on people you converse with on a daily basis?
- Are you doing any legacy activities? Creating things that will outlive you to teach what you know and value to future generations?
- What does your dream day look like?

Once you have clarified those desires, brainstorm how you can make that happen. How could this dream day be every day of your life? And if you're going to get bored with that, then add in things that keep you on your toes and not bored.

If your day was perfect, what would it look like? And then, how can you make that happen?

Making our dreams a reality required steps which meant "breaking" and rebuilding our current business model to support those desires. Here's what some of our steps looked like:

1. We took 22 of our perfectly good online courses off the market in order to focus on the programs that would allow us greater impact and time freedom.
2. We added live events to our marketing strategy allowing us to reach and teach more people in group settings.
3. We blocked off most Fridays and Monday mornings on the calendar for family time.
4. We began outsourcing the busy work that kept us from our best work, and training/hiring people to support us.
5. We chose to call work "business activities" to reframe it as something positive we get to do.
6. We chose to invest in programs, communities and mentors who could wisely advise and encourage us.

Once you define it, you can work for it. You can refine it and set goals. You can make tweaks to your routines and commitments to get yourself closer and closer to the goal.

Here are some questions that will help brainstorm the steps needed to make your dream day happen:
What do I need to do to get to where this is possible?
What action steps do I need to take?
What decisions do I need to make?
What changes do I need to make?
What do I need to let go of or stop doing?
What help do I need to hire?
What do I need to learn?
What training do I need to take?
Is there something I need to give up in my schedule or in my life to make this possible?

Set all of that out before you. Determine what is the first step and then the next step etc, towards making it happen.

You can also go through the same process for other areas of your life:
What do you want your marriage to look like?
What do you want your friendships to look like?
What do you want your relationships with your kids to look like?
What do you want your finances to look like?
What do you want your health/fitness to look like?
What do you want your home to look like?
What do you want your legacy to look like? What will be left behind that makes a difference into the future?

Today Tap and I have the team and business we've dreamed of, an AirBnB space finished and listed online.[38] When we're home we start each day with quiet time and coffee in the hammock chair on the porch. We work three and a half days a week from wherever we want to. We have bountiful invitations to speak in both ministry and business circles, and we are thoroughly enjoying the adolescent and teen years of discipleship and fellowship with our children. So when that gratefulness alarm goes off each morning, I do praise Him, with all my heart!

As it is written, "I have made you the father of many nations"—in the presence of the God in whom he believed, who gives life to the dead and calls into existence the things that do not exist. Romans 4:17 ESV

Does the dream stop now? No. Now that we're seeing these desires come into existence, God is awakening even bigger dreams in us and we're now making plans for the next steps He's putting before us.

Your clarity, vision, and purpose give you faith to say: *"This is what God has for me."* That in turn helps you make decisions and take action to achieve it.

If something comes as an opportunity for you, you can say, *"That doesn't fit with the goal I have right now, and so I will put it on the back burner,"* or *"I will say 'no' for a time because it doesn't fit the direction I'm going in this moment (or for this month, or for this quarter, or whatever it is), to meet this next big goal I believe God wants me to set for myself or for my business."*

It may not be a bad idea. It may be a fantastic opportunity, but if it doesn't fit with the goals God has aligned you with right now, then you can say no with freedom. You are less likely to have guilt around saying no because it doesn't fit with what God has in front of you right now. When you know the no will help you reach the goal faster it's because the purpose and vision have given you clarity and freedom in your business and you are more likely to let nothing distract you or pull you aside from going in the right direction.

Aligning your expectations and goals with the vision God's planted inside of you is much like purposing in your heart, as Daniel did, not to "defile yourself with the King's meat." (Daniel 1:8)

Daniel had a vision. He had clarity about what was expected of him and what his goals were. He also had expectations that God would honor what He'd put in his heart and Daniel wasn't going to let anything pull him away from that desire. That's what God wants for you too.

God places desires in you to meet those goals, as well as challenges He knows will grow you into who you are becoming in Christ.

We humans are motivated by having purpose, by pressing towards a vision and an expected result. You will find success when you're willing to let God define it, refine it and show you His vision for business success through the alignment of the abilities and desires He has given you with His Word and the leading of the Holy Spirit.

For Reflection:

My biggest takeaway from this chapter is....

The truth I need to believe and act on is...

My action will be...

I will take this action on/by (date)...

20. Keep Your Plans CURRENT & FLEXIBLE

A man's heart deviseth his way: but the Lord directeth his steps.

Proverbs 16:9

When we moved to Mexico over 15 years ago, we thought we'd be in that first ministry for the rest of our lives. Two years later God began moving us to another ministry that we'd have never considered if we hadn't already been in the first one. Nine months into the second ministry, there was another plot twist and from there we moved through several church plant ministries while building our business for the next decade or so. At each stop on the journey, we made plans, evaluated, pivoted, tweaked... Tap and I are so grateful God was directing the steps that ultimately led to where we are today.

Every time Tap and I sit down for our quarterly business planning session, every time the month rolls over and I get to set out the new goals for this month, I think of Proverbs 16:9:

A man's heart deviseth his way: but the Lord directeth his steps.

It's my job as the CEO of this business to apply myself to instruction and learn what I need to know to do my job well. It's my job to ask for wisdom of God, and get sound counsel and advice from trusted coaches and mentors.

It's my job to take what I have in my hands and make the best plans I know how to make for marketing and growing this business to meet the goals God's set before us, but... in all of that, I have to acknowledge that God is God. He is sovereign. He is all-knowing. He is already in tomorrow. And I have to yield my plans and my calendar to His control, just as I yield to Him the results of my efforts.

"How do you do that?" you ask. You set goals, design action steps to meet the goals and then implement. Evaluating and iterating at each step.

Here are some questions we use when planning:
Outcome:
What is the goal?
How will you know you've met the goal?
Why is it important to reach the goal?
What is the biggest potential hindrance to you meeting this goal?
What can you do to avoid that hindrance or make it a non-issue?
What's the result if you don't meet it?
What is the result if the goal is met?
What, if anything, needs to be set aside to focus on the goal?

Resources:
What further information do you need to be successful?

What resources do you have to meet the goal?
What resources do you need?
How can other people help you find the needed resources?
Who do you know who could possibly help?

Process:
What steps need to be taken?
By whom?
On what dates?
What statistics or information do you need to track as you work toward the goal?
What will you do as a reward? for yourself? for the team?
When will you celebrate?

As a teenager, I fell in love with the nostalgic silver ring that's made out of a spoon handle. My aunt had one, and it just seemed the epitome of "fancy" and "unique" to me, but I never had the opportunity to get one for myself. So, when I published the book, *In Spite of Myself: How Intentional Praise Can Transform Your Heart and Home*[39], the goal in my heart was to get that book to the bestseller list on Amazon and reward myself with a spoon ring. It wasn't a completely unselfish goal either because I'd been rejected by a big name Christian publishing agent who told me no one would ever buy this book.

I knew God wanted this message to get out though, and I was determined to do my part. And seeing God do something people said couldn't be done would be really amazing too! The ring only cost about fifteen dollars, so it was not super extravagant, yet the perfect extra incentive to make it to the bestseller list with this book.

During the 12-week launch process God miraculously brought together a team of 150 people. And I don't know how He did it. It defeated all the numbers, statistics and probabilities that authors usually have to reach, but the Lord took that book to the bestseller list in the first week on Amazon, and completely blew the stats out of the water!

Every time I wear that silver spoon ring I am reminded that God can do the impossible, that God can do things exceeding abundantly above what you could ask, think, dream or even dare imagine (Ephesians 3:20).

Don't be afraid to set goals, expect big things and plan the celebration. Celebrate and to give God glory!

And if He changes the plan mid-stream with His divine appointments or new information that make it evident He's leading a different way, don't balk at it. Be willing to pivot, knowing that His way is perfect.

As for God, his way is perfect: the word of the Lord is tried: he is a buckler to all those that trust in him. Psalm 18;30

Yield your interruptions to God
and learn to see them as
His divine appointments.

Sometimes "interruptions" (divine appointments) become our biggest blessings as we choose to see God's sovereignty over them as well.

Like the Sunday my youngest was ill and not able to go to church. I was really looking forward to the service that week and a bit upset by the fact that we had to miss. As I sat on her bed reading books and talking with her the conversations turned spiritual, and before lunch she'd given her life to Christ. What a blessing in disguise that day's sickness was.

Or the time I stepped out of a conference session to make a business call and another attendee intercepted me and began talking about his work, which led to the normal pleasantries of where are you from? Which led to the fact that we came to México as missionaries, which led into a full half hour exchange of fact and fiction around what a relationship with God and eternal security truly is. No one had ever challenged this young man's beliefs with the truth from God's Word before. He didn't accept Christ that day, but that seeming interruption was most definitely a divine appointment in which a seed was planted.

For as the rain cometh down, and the snow from heaven, and returneth not thither, but watereth the earth, and maketh it bring forth and bud, that it may give seed to the sower, and bread to the eater: So shall my word be that goeth forth out of my mouth: it shall not return unto me void, but it shall accomplish that which I please, and it shall prosper in the thing whereto I sent it. Isaiah 55:10-12

We often think of time as something that works against us, but really time, just like money, is a tool you get to use as you steward this business. The difference is you can always get more of the tool of money, but you'll never get this moment back once it's spent. Be sensitive to how God is directing your time and interruptions.

Often the struggle is not so much in managing time as it is managing priorities, yielding to God's purposes, and exercising the "No" muscle.

Saying no to the good in favor of the best.
Saying no to distractions to focus on what will get you to the goal.
Saying no to overcommitting and people pleasing so you have time to honor your most important priorities.

In the mastermind group I coach we have read the book *Deep Work*, by Cal Newport[40]. The idea of this book is that the reason that you don't have time for the things that are important (in life or in business) is you have over-committed to things that are not important but you can't set them aside to focus on those things that are supposed to be priorities. You are over-committed.

Managing your no's is your first line of defense. Some call it evaluating the "opportunity cost". You can ask yourself, *"Does this opportunity line up with the stated goals for the business?"* If not, then this is not the time. Another question that gives great clarity as to opportunity cost is "*What am I saying no to if I say yes to this opportunity?"*

The reason you must set goals and map out your plan is so that you know what you're supposed to be focused on. If a wonderful opportunity presents itself, you can then go back to The Owner with the plan and ask, *"Okay, God, does this line up with the goals that you had me set for this week/*

month/quarter?" If not, then you get to say, *"No, I am choosing not to do that right now to stay focused on the stated goal and give it the attention that it needs."*

Remember, every no doesn't necessarily mean no forever. It just means no right now. That is true whether you're asking something and you receive a no or whether someone is asking of you and you get to give a no. Saying no is a muscle that must be built to protect the goals of God's work. Saying no can be very freeing for you because you have the confidence of the goals and the things that God has set before you as priorities. Compare your opportunities to the set goals and if it doesn't align, then you don't need to do it, or at least not right now.

All of your thoughts and your actions are based on what you believe and what you think. Time ~~management~~ investment then begins in your heart. It starts with what you believe.

Proper time ~~management~~ investment begins in your heart.

If you believe God does all things well, and if you believe God has given you a sound mind and the ability to manage the things He's put in your hand well, then He can help you handle time management too. If you need His wisdom, all you have to do is ask (James 1:9). And if you need His help, He promises to do through you the things He's called you to do (1 Thessalonians 5:24). You really are set up for success from day one!

When we started our businesses after being in full-time ministry for several years, many people wondered how we could possibly have time to do ministry and business and home educate our children?

We found that the Lord multiplied our time because He had called us to it and He gave us even more opportunities to minister to others through the business He gave us. I can't explain it except that I know He's also multiplied loaves and fishes when there was a need for it in order to get a message to the people who needed the message (Matthew 14, Mark 6, Luke 9, John 6). I believe God can work miracles with time, money, health and physical things when we yield them to Him and it accomplishes His purposes.

Time management starts with what do I believe about God, about the time and tasks that He has given me.

To get a handle on time management, after evaluating your beliefs, you next need to evaluate your tasks. What do you have on your plate right now? It's sobering, but I want you to take time to think through what your commitments are right now. How many roles are you filling on a weekly basis? How many daily or weekly tasks do you have? Write them down. Yours may look different, but my roles include:

- wife
- mother
- daughter
- sister
- aunt
- friend

- teacher
- coach
- business owner
- director of marketing
- copy writer
- podcaster
- speaker
- graphic designer
- neighbor
- church member
- menu planner
- household manager
- curriculum planner
- record keeper
- house keeper
- Etc.

Then under each of those roles, add the daily or weekly tasks you complete in each role. Go ahead. Put your bookmark in here and make a list.

Got your list? Great. Now, look at your list and evaluate which of those tasks are God given assignments? and which would you say you are taking on yourself?

Next, I want you to go through and cross off the ones that you know you need to get rid of and circle the ones you could delegate to someone else. These are things you know you don't even need to pray about, because you know that you're not supposed to be doing it. Get those things off the list.

You do need to keep your word and you need to have integrity even in the way you cancel those commitments. However, it can be done. As for wisdom, ask your mentor, spouse or a friend to help you figure out how you can reduce your commitment with integrity or delegate that task to somebody else who can be responsible for it. God will give you wisdom to get those things off your plate.

Next, mark the ones that you think you need to get rid of, but you're not sure about. Ask God for clarity. He will give you clarity about what does not need to be on your plate. Narrow down the things you don't need to do. Even good things become bad if they distract us, or if they keep us from doing the main things that God wants us to do.

For instance, I was in the middle of an online business class and the opportunity came up to take a second one. I knew I needed the second one, but wouldn't be able to give adequate time to both, so I said "No for now." I finished the first class and the next time the second class enrollment opened I could embrace it and focus on excelling in applying that content to my business. I was focused on one thing at a time, both intellectually and financially, whereas if I'd done both at once, it would have added stress in both areas.

Time, as well as money and energies, must be invested wisely to yield the expected return, and that takes planning and intention.

You don't manage time, money, or energies. You invest them.

It is possible for you to be busy and yet so distracted that you're not getting anything done well. The power of *The 12 Week Year*,[41] by Brian Moran is also the idea behind the *Flamingo Biz Quarterly Planner*[42]. These two books, when used together, can help you learn to focus on completing those short-term goals that contribute to the success of the long-term goals.

You are much more effective in the short term when focused on a few main goals than if you are focused on ten different long-term goals and trying to do a little on each of them all at the same time.

Focusing on short-term goals, allows you to focus on one main goal and give it your full concentration. When you can get it done and move on to the next thing, you're much more effective and productive than if your time was distracted between everything you're trying to get done in a long-term plan.

For example, our business set a goal for the number of people we want to enroll in our *Master Teacher Accelerator*™ program[43] this year. Recently we embarked on a fairly involved video marketing campaign to help us reach prospective clients across four video platforms. We determined what our goal was and what actions we thought we needed to take to get there. We identified the important data points to track and committed the time and resources to make it happen. By tracking the results monthly, at the end of the quarter we had enough data to inform us as to our next course of action.

Our data clearly showed that two platforms were outperforming the others in gaining viewers, converting viewers to subscribers and subscribers to client leads. With that information, we were able to adjust the plan for the following quarter to do less on the platforms that didn't show results and re-allocate the resources from those platforms to do even more on the ones that were working. (Side note: if you are enjoying this book, you can subscribe to our YouTube channel for weekly educational and inspirational videos to help you keep growing your business. www.youtube.com/c/KatieHornorHandprintLegacy)

My point is not to suggest you use any one specific platform, it's to encourage you to test which platforms work for you and *your* people. It sounds like common sense - but do you do it? Do you plan with intention or just post randomly to look or feel busy without a real sense of how this activity contributes to your goals? It's important to continually be tracking, evaluating, tweaking and iterating on the plan with the current wisdom available to best reach the goals set before you. In this instance, it involved a 'no' for publishing so often on one of the platforms that I personally enjoy creating content for. But the data said it wasn't contributing to the stated goal for this time.

You may not always personally "like" the best decision. There may be people who disagree with your decision. Saying 'no' might offend someone sometimes, so do be gracious, especially with team members you are shepherding, but don't surprised when it happens. People may accuse you of being lazy. They may say you are uncaring. Some may even go so far as to say you are in sin if you don't do what they're expecting you to do. However, if you are walking humbly with your God, you can walk with your head held high in confidence that you're pleasing Him. He will lead in your decisions, in your commitments and in your saying 'no' when it's necessary.

On the flip side, I also want to encourage you to be aware of God's still small voice telling you what you're supposed to be doing even when it goes *against* the logical data.

- It didn't make logical sense to Noah to build an ark. (Genesis 6)
- It didn't make logical sense to Moses to lead all these people into an overflowing Sea. (Exodus 14)
- It didn't make logical sense to walk around a city Joshua was supposed to be attacking. (Joshua 6)
- It didn't make logical sense to Gideon to take only a few hundred men to fight the enemy. (Judges 7)
- It didn't make logical sense to David to not start on building the Temple. (1 Chronicles 28)
- It didn't make logical sense to Naaman to go wash in a dirty river. (2 Kings 5)
- It didn't make logical sense to the man lame for 38 years to try to stand and walk. (John 5)
- It didn't make logical sense to the neighbors to let Jesus pray over a girl who'd already been pronounced dead. (Mark 5)

Need I go on?

When you're so busy and so distracted that you have no time to listen for His voice, or to stop and think that you need to ask Him about a decision, then you're too busy.

You may have to cancel some commitments, and people may be offended. You cannot control their response and neither are you held responsible for it, but do what you need to do to make the space in your life to hear from God about your business and marketing decisions. You must know and obey the voice of God, and know that you are pleasing Him with your decisions, even when it means saying no.

Someone who does not have your relationship with God may not understand. They are not you. They should not be judging you, and don't get trapped into judging them because they shouldn't be judging you. That just creates a vicious cycle and no one gets anywhere. Determine in your heart that you won't let it bother you. Don't take it personally. Walk tall in the confidence of what you know God wants you to do because you're going to answer for you, not for anyone else and the rewards are going to be glorious.

For Reflection:

My biggest takeaway from this chapter is....

The truth I need to believe and act on is...

My action will be...

I will take this action on/by (date)...

21. Engage & INVEST WITH INTENTION

For which of you, intending to build a tower, sitteth not down first, and counteth the cost, whether he have sufficient to finish it? Lest haply, after he hath laid the foundation, and is not able to finish it, all that behold it begin to mock him, Saying, This man began to build, and was not able to finish.
Luke 14:28-30

No force save God can make time stand still or create more time. Time once invested can never be refunded. You can always make more of the tool of money, but time is the most precious of the tools you get to steward here on earth. Scripture says it passes as if it were a shadow:

All the days of his vain life which he spendeth as a shadow? for who can tell a man what shall be after him under the sun? Ecclesiastes 6:12

Time is the most precious of the tools you get to steward here on earth.

I think this is why I so dislike sleeping. I understand the physical need for rest, but there is so much to do and so much to be said... I sometimes feel like it's a waste of time to sleep. When I have the privilege to attend in person events, I love staying up late to talk with people. I'll even get up early to meet people before a session. I always feel like *"I can sleep later, but I've only got these 36 hours to impact and be impacted by these people and I don't want to miss a moment of it!"*

I do believe that using every available moment for something can be a danger however... Don't be the person who is so busy you can't even have dinner with your family, send an encouraging note to a friend or client, or stop to listen to your child's latest exciting discovery. Don't be the one who always has an activity, or something on the calendar, and if you don't, you're looking for something to fill that space.

In my experience, people might fill up the calendar with busy-ness because they're afraid to do the thing they know God wants them to do and so they stay too busy to do it fearing that if they get quiet He'll convict them about it. I'm not saying that's the case every time, but speaking from personal experience...

For example: You have a deadline looming, so what do you do? Everything but the thing you're supposed to be doing. Am I right? We do everything: *"Oh look, my bed needs to be made."* *"Oh look, nobody did the laundry yet today. I need to go do that."* *"Oh dear, that errand got overlooked. I need to take care of this right now."* Even though it's not technically time sensitive and may not even be a personal responsibility...

When you have a deadline, and it seems like everything else is more important, could it be because you are afraid of getting it done? You need to find the root of the problem and replace the belief with right beliefs, right thoughts and right actions. You need to sit down and figure out what the next right step is, and commit to doing it.

In Matthew 25, the story is told of a master who gave his 3 servants differing amounts of money. The servant who received the most went out quickly and took action. Perhaps he had the most experience and knew that he had a small window of opportunity. Perhaps he understood that time is short, and we must redeem it and invest it wisely (Ephesians 5:16).

You and I need to act, not sit frozen in fear, hoarding the resources we manage like the third servant did. He was reprimanded for not getting a return on the investment and lost the privilege of managing it altogether.

What is that thing you're afraid of? A risk you know you need to take to grow your business, an investment you need to make of time or money, a conversation you need to have with a friend or team member, a change you need to make...

Why are you afraid of it? Go deeper.
Why are you afraid of that? Go deeper.
Why are you afraid of that? Go deep and keep going as deep as you can. Keep asking why.

I've heard it recommended to go as many as seven questions deep for why you are afraid of doing something, or why you believe a certain thing to uncover the real belief.

Then identify the false belief holding you captive and attack the root problem and false belief of that fear with truth from God's Word. It's not for nothing "*Do not fear*" appears in some form in the Bible more than 365 times[44]. That's one for every day of the year!

Committing to take action
is an investment of intention.

Is it a fear of man? Is it fear of success? Is it fear of change and unknown? Is it a lack of knowledge? What is it?

Committing to take action is an investment of intention to complete that thing and cross it off your list, giving you freedom to move to the next project or goal in front of you.

And if the procrastination is because the situation has changed and that task is no longer needed, relevant or important, give yourself permission to let it go and move on to what is important.

If the enemy can keep you distracted,
he can keep you debilitated.

When you allow yourself to fill your life with busy-ness to distract you from the one thing that you need to be doing, it diminishes the power of the time you have available to do the work God has called you to.

Luke chapter ten tells the story of Martha and Mary. You may have heard this over and over and over again, but I want you to think about it from the aspect of being so busy that you don't have the time *not* to do that one key thing right now.

As they went on their way, Jesus entered a village and a woman named Martha welcomed Him into her house, and she had a sister called Mary who sat at the Lord's feet and listened to his teaching, but Martha was distracted with much serving. Luke 10:38-40 (ESV)

It is actually translated distracted in the ESV version.

And (Martha) came to him (Jesus), and said, Lord, dost thou not care that my sister hath left me to serve alone? bid her therefore that she help me. And Jesus answered and said unto her, Martha, Martha, thou art careful and troubled about many things: But one thing is needful: and Mary hath chosen that good part, which shall not be taken away from her. Luke 10:40-42

Martha was busy serving. She was so busy serving that she was completely distracted–from what? From the one thing she should have been doing, sitting at Jesus' feet.

Mary was sitting at His feet. Martha was in the other room. She was all over the house. She was welcoming, serving, loving on people...

I want you to hear that part–Martha was *loving* on people, and even that was a distraction from what she should have been doing at that minute, which was sitting at Jesus' feet.

How many times do you and I get so busy even doing "good things" that we are distracted from sitting at His feet, from learning about Him, from knowing Him and what He wants us to do? If Martha had known God, if she had been close enough to hear His voice in that moment, she would have known that the most important thing was learning of Him, and getting to know Him so that when He was not at her house teaching, she could serve those people better, love them more and meet their needs better. Her investment of time in service, diminished the returns that could have been hers. Don't let yourself be so distracted by being busy for God that you neglect *knowing* Christ, for that is the one thing with the biggest return for your time.

It's in knowing Him you learn He doesn't want you to be afraid. He is with you. He is your judge and He gives you the grace (divine enablement) to love others without judgment. And when you're loving and serving others, God is your counselor. He is the One you run to when you have a problem. He is the One with all the answers, the One who knows you inside and out. God wants you to go to Him with your problems. He is the One that can give you knowledge and wisdom and understanding even down to the tiniest details of where to invest your time, finances and focus.

Being confident of this very thing, that he which hath begun a good work in you will perform it until the day of Jesus Christ. Philippians 1:6

The work God is doing in your life as the CEO of this business, and the work He's doing in your clients through you are investments. Not to be confused with costs, investments are the things you have an ongoing relationship with and expect a return from.

You will have both costs and investments in business, marketing being one of them. To steward God's resources wisely, you must be cognizant of which is which.

I like to think of the costs as things that are here today and gone tomorrow. Whereas investments are things that will continue to work towards the goals God has set before us.

In practical marketing terms, a cost might be a social media scheduling tool. A small expense that saves you time in getting your message in front of people today. Those are generally low monthly fees at fixed rates and have certain features or benefits. It might also be a stock photo or video subscription that provides content for your marketing designs and videos or payment processing fees you pay in order to accept online payments from clients. That's the cost of doing business.

An investment might be a VIP day, like the ones we offer to our clients, to gain knowledge and strategy to help you reach your 1 year or 5 year goals. Or it might be an investment to create a book, promotional video or docu-series about your business whose shelf life will allow the message to keep reaching people long after you publish it.

As the CEO created in the image of your Creator God, you have been given dominion over all the earth:

And God said, Let us make man in our image, after our likeness: and let them have dominion over the fish of the sea, and over the fowl of the air, and over the cattle, and over all the earth, and over every creeping thing that creepeth upon the earth. Genesis 1:26

You have time, money, people, connections, material things, digital tools, courses, coaches, apps and potentially even a garden and animals at your disposal...

Grace and peace be multiplied unto you through the knowledge of God, and of Jesus our Lord, According as his divine power hath given unto us all things that pertain unto life and godliness, through the knowledge of him that hath called us to glory and virtue. 2 Peter 2:1-2

All things have been given to you to use in the work of the Lord. And He's asked you to be "fruitful" with it. To multiply it. To invest what you've been given for a return...

And God blessed them, and God said unto them, Be fruitful, and multiply, and replenish the earth, and subdue it: and have dominion over the fish of the sea, and over the fowl of the air, and over every living thing that moveth upon the earth. Genesis 1:28

And John 15 says you "bear fruit" by abiding in Him:

Abide in me, and I in you. As the branch cannot bear fruit of itself, except it abide in the vine; no more can ye, except ye abide in me. I am the vine, ye are the branches: He that abideth in me, and I in him, the same bringeth forth much fruit: for without me ye can do nothing. John 15:4-5

Fear thou not; for I am with thee: be not dismayed; for I am thy God: I will strengthen thee; yea, I will help thee; yea, I will uphold thee with the right hand of my righteousness. Isaiah 41:10

Jesus said unto him, If thou canst believe, all things are possible to him that believeth. Mark 9:23

God is with You. He's with you in your business. He's with you in your home, in your car and at events you attend. It doesn't matter where you are. The Lord is always with you if you choose to walk with Him, and that means you have all you need to engage and invest your resources well.

For Reflection:

My biggest takeaway from this chapter is....

The truth I need to believe and act on is...

My action will be...

I will take this action on/by (date)...

22. Treasure YOUR PEOPLE

And now abideth faith, hope, charity, these three;
but the greatest of these is charity (love in action).
1 Corinthians 13:13

One of my favorite songs from the 1945 musical *State Fair*[45] is "It's a Grand Night for Singing" performed by Dick Haymes in which he sings:

♪♪ *Maybe it's more than the moon. Maybe it's more than the birds,*
Maybe it's more than sight of the night, in a light too lovely for words.
Maybe it's more than the earth shiny in silvery blue.
Maybe the reason I'm feeling this way has something to do with you! ♪♪

The reason your people, your clients and customers will feel the way they do about you has something to do with *you*!

It's more than the way you have your video lighting set up. It's more than the backgrounds you use or the graphics you so carefully create. It's more than the colors, logos and taglines on your website.

Your people are drawn to *you*. The authentic you. The you who is so passionate that they get success with their problem that you've built an entire business around helping them! The you who cares more about their success than about making the sale. The you who loves them and sees God's potential for them. The you who believes in their success until they can believe it for themselves. The you who prays for them as Jesus prayed for us:

I pray for them: I pray not for the world, but for them which thou hast given me; for they are thine. John 17:1-26

The you who obsesses (in a good way) over how to reach them and how to help them succeed, so they can be all they were created to be, and do what God created them to do in the world.

And now abideth faith, hope, charity, these three; but the greatest of these is charity (love in action). 1 Corinthians 13:13

Jesus said unto him, Thou shalt love the Lord thy God with all thy heart, and with all thy soul, and with all thy mind. This is the first and great commandment. And

the second is like unto it, Thou shalt love thy neighbour as thyself.
Matthew 22:37-39

Why is love the greatest of these? The greatest commandment?

For God so loved the world, that he gave his only begotten Son, that whosoever believeth in him should not perish, but have everlasting life. John 3:16

Love is the greatest of these because love changed the world, and continues to change the world.

Our big vision at our company, Handprint Legacy, is to see the world become a place where the coaching programs and course businesses that belong to people of God would be the standard of excellence and the beloved first choice in the marketplace at large, because of the way you do business, because of the way your course or program changes their lives, because of the way you love the people you serve and the people you come into contact with. That your legacy would outlive you and continue to be a guiding mark impacting future generations because of how you let God love the world through you.

When you are living personally in alignment with the greatest commandments of God, you cannot help but spill that over into the business activities you get to do.

Jesus didn't give the disciples a roadmap. He gave them an invitation to follow him. He said, *"Follow me, learn from me, do what I do, learn how I walk with the Father. You walk with me and learn from me and do what I do."* When they did this, they found a relationship with Him, and an increased audience to hear the message. They found increased opportunities and new titles. They were given new goals in the Kingdom and new definitions of success. They had increased reward, and they created a generational legacy.

How many of those disciples do you think who grew up in a sleepy little fishermen's town looked forward to the future and said, *"You know what, 2,000 years from now, I bet people are still going to be talking about me."* I guarantee you, not a single one. Yet that's exactly what we are doing.

God blessed them with an impact that spanned generations because they were willing to follow Him. They believed Him and were willing to walk with Him. They were willing to love the unlovable. They were willing to give His message to whoever God brought to them in their daily walk and daily work.

I was blessed to grow up next door to my inventor and visionary Grandpa. He had a tremendous passion tell to others about Jesus. He was always tinkering on some project or other, but he would never do them by himself. When you walked in the door he'd say *"Oh there you are!"* as if he'd been waiting all day just for you, and then he'd say, *"Come help me do this."* It could be a grandkid, one of his sons visiting, a neighbor, whoever was there. It didn't matter. *"Come help me work on this."* He always had a project he "needed" a hand with.

Now that I'm an adult, I realize it was never about the project. I was the project.

You use the work to create the relationship which creates an opportunity to speak truth into another's life and point them to Jesus.

As we worked my Grandpa would talk to me about God. He would teach me truths of who God is. He would explain Scripture to me and remind me of God's goodness and His sovereignty. One of his favorite things to say was *"Remember, Katie, God is not surprised."*

The legacy of his words and example has impacted my parenting and how I work and interact with my team and clients. Now I see projects as opportunities for relationships and Kingdom conversations of legacy impact. My projects aren't greasy motors and hydraulic presses. They look more like helping a client build out a content outline for a coaching package, mapping out the experience piece of someone's high ticket enrollment event or debriefing the results of a course launch email campaign, but the purpose is the same: to treasure the people I get to interact with and impact them for the Gospel with every opportunity I have.

That's what God is asking you to do, too. Regardless of the niche or the specific business that God has you working in, your mission is to glorify the Father and to point others to Him and His redeeming love while you work. And when you do that, your work really can be your *best* worship.

For Reflection:

My biggest takeaway from this chapter is....

The truth I need to believe and act on is...

My action will be...

I will take this action on/by (date)...

23. Live IN AWE

Then said I, Woe is me! for I am undone; because I am a man of unclean lips,
and I dwell in the midst of a people of unclean lips:
for mine eyes have seen the King, the Lord of hosts.
Isaiah 6:5

Grasping even the full power of even the most practical aspects of your business does not happen until you walk in the fear of the Lord. Until you know who God is, what He's capable of, and how it applies to you personally, you cannot apply those truths to your business.

Mardi Collier and her husband Ken are Directors at the Christian camp I served at during my summers in college. Her book *What Do I Know About My God?* has been one of the most impactful books in my adult life. In it she says: *"We have to make numerous daily choices about whether we want to live life God's way or please ourselves and do it our way. Since life is all about God and not about us, we should live all of life in the light of what we know about Him.*

Who He is should affect how we think and the way we live. We can't make right choices if we don't know Him." [46]

When you are walking with God, you can choose rightly and God promises reward. When you're not choosing to apply His laws in His ways, there ultimately will not be God's success in what you're doing.

The fear of God means that your actions and words are not dictated by what others will think of you, but by what God thinks of you. It means you are more concerned about God's feelings than man's feelings, more concerned about God's approval, than man's approval, more concerned about God's praise than man's praise.

When you are letting the fear of man rule you, when you are living in the fear of what others will say, and not as concerned about God, ultimately, that becomes an idol in your life. An idol is anything that takes that primary worship position in your life (Exodus 20:3). If you're spending more time thinking about what other people are going to think and say, and letting their opinions mold your actions, your responses and decisions, then their approval has become an idol.

The only one whose approval you need is the Lord's. And it took me until I was nearly into my forties to finally grasp the truth of that one thing. God's opinion is the only one that carries eternal weight, the only one whose permission and approval is needed.

And by fear I don't mean being afraid of Him, but the fear that is a kind of reverential awe. The thing that inspires, scares and blows your mind to think that God is so awesome, so big and so powerful, and yet He cares so deeply about every little detail in your life and business and marketing plans.

It's the kind of fear that says, *"I may fear negative opinions of other people and what they might say about me, but I know God is bigger than that, and I know God has called me to this. He can handle anything that might happen."* That's the fear or the awe of God that we're talking about here.

This kind of awe helps us see with clarity what that next step is. It's the kind of fear that says, *"Okay, in this instance, I don't see the next step. Even though I can't see where I'm stepping, I'm going to have faith in my God to take that next right step, because I know He's called me to this."*

Tap and I have lived where fear of man is big, where you are given jobs to do, and then micromanaged. If you don't get approval for every little step along the way, it is always wrong. We smiled through our fears, but we lived fearful.

Fear of man became ingrained in us to the point that we were often immobilized by the fear of being shamed, afraid of retribution and criticism. Because it hurt and felt like that's all we ever got.

When the Lord brought us to Campeche, Mexico and to the stage where we were doing ministry more on our own, following the Lord's guidance, we still fought that overarching feeling of fear that someone was going to be upset with us at each decision we made. Fought the lie that anything that brought us joy might somehow land us "in trouble" with someone else.

We had been conditioned by humans in ministry to believe we had to please man to "deserve" to keep doing ministry, and we'd also experienced the hurt of people having betrayed us and lost belief in us.

Living that way had actually created neurological brain patterns of thought and behavior and for a while we lost our understanding of who God is. Human approval had become an idol to the point that every decision we made came down to *"What are the supporters going to say? How are they going to respond to this?"*

When God revealed to us how unhealthy and anti-biblical these beliefs were, we had to work to establish a new thought pattern of asking *"Who is my God? Is He bigger than this? Has He called me to this? Can He take care of my needs, no matter what people say? no matter who might discontinue financial support?"*

And the answer was always a resounding YES!
And that, my friend, is your answer too.

That answer and the knowledge that God built our brains so that they can be retrained; those patterns and connections can be corrected and "made new" with truth - this always fills me with awe.

God is bigger.
Bigger than your problems.

Bigger than your fears.

Bigger than your finances.

Bigger than your "competition."

Bigger than your unbelief.

Bigger than you health issues.

Bigger than the positive and negative people in your life.

Bigger than every obstacle you face.

God is bigger. And that should inspire you with awe.

"You do what you do and you say what you say because you think what you think. You think what you think because you believe what you believe about God and His Word and yourself."[47]

If your beliefs are not correct, then your thinking is not correct. Additionally, your words, actions and reactions will also not be in alignment with God, His Word or His will for your life and business.

Your business decisions, your marketing plans, the actions you take all stem from the beliefs of your heart. Everything you do is influenced by those beliefs.

God has all power, He's strong enough to protect you. So, can He give you His strength when you need it? Yes, He can.

God has all power and He's always with you, so do you need to go through life afraid? No, you don't.

God is your judge. He's created you for this work and put you into the position of CEO on purpose, promising to do the work through you. So, do you need to make business decisions in fear of other people's judgments, reactions or responses? No, you don't. (1 Thessalonians 5:24).

God is good all the time, in all circumstances, with no evil in Him at all, and He is always good with pure motives, and has all power to control. So good in fact, you can trust that whatever He ordains or allows in your life or business is for a good purpose (Romans 8:28).

Do you see where this is going? Do you see how knowing Him makes such a difference as it filters down to your daily business and marketing decisions, based on your belief system?

If you believe God is all knowing (omniscient), and all powerful (omnipotent), and always present (omnipresent), and all good and always good (omni benevolent), then doesn't it make sense that you can trust Him?

Good doesn't equal easy. When I say that God is all good, I don't mean to say that you're going to have an easy life because you believe in Him. I do mean to say that when you know your God as all powerful, all knowing, all present and all good, you have a much greater freedom and confidence to walk in His love and share His love and transformative truth with the people in your life and in your business than if you were operating out of fear and doubt.

Thus saith the Lord, Let not the wise man glory in his wisdom, neither let the mighty man glory in his might, let not the rich man glory in his riches: But let him that glorieth glory in this, that he understandeth and knoweth me, that I am the Lord which exercise lovingkindness, judgment, and righteousness, in the earth: for in these things I delight, saith the Lord. Jeremiah 9:23-24

Your definitions of business, marketing and success are going to look different from my definitions. They likely will look different from every other person who reads this book. But the one thing they will have in common is the connection to our God.

When you understand and know the Lord, you are successful because you know who He is and what He expects of you, it gives you the freedom to serve Him with all your heart. That freedom is what will ultimately bring the things that you will consider true success in your life.

Success is not a number. It's not a dollar sign. It's not an accomplishment. Every time you reach a goal you feel good for a minute and then you're on to the next thing because success is not a definitive definition.

God is saying *"If you will glory in anything, if there is any honor, if there is any triumph, it's because you know me and you understand my ways and what I want for you."*

Knowing is being in relationship with… It's spending time communicating, listening and sharing what we're going through in our daily lives, laughing together, talking together, giving, expressing gratitude and praise, enjoying part of another's life. That is what God wants from you. He wants that relationship where you know Him so intimately that He can be part of every aspect of your life.

I hope by now you have seen that just like the flamingo, who you are on the inside is going to show on the outside. You are saved to good works inside and out. You can't separate your faith (who you are) from what you do.

And because you have Christ in you, you're not going to beat people over the head with the fact that you're a Christian and you are consulting God's opinion on your decisions for your business. However, it is going to be obvious by the light in your eyes, by the love in your heart, by the care of your service and the value you offer that you are different.

The daily life part of your faith cannot be separated from your business.

That should be the thing that draws them in and makes them want to do business with you. You will display the character, integrity and love for people that makes them desire to do business with you.

If you don't truly know God, you will believe the lies that Satan tells you and try as. you. might to come across as one of His, people will see through it.

People are trained to recognize counterfeit bills by learning to recognize the truth. They study the true, authentic bills. They memorize every single detail of a true bill so when they see a fake, they instantly spot the difference. And when countries (like México where I live) come out with newly designed currency every decade or so that can make it harder.

You need to know God so well, know His truth backwards and forwards so that when you face a lie of the enemy, or a new version of it, you can immediately spot it for what it is, cast it out and have nothing to do with it.

For the weapons of our warfare are not carnal, but mighty through God to the pulling down of strong holds;) Casting down imaginations, and every high thing that exalteth itself against the knowledge of God, and bringing into captivity every thought to the obedience of Christ. 2 Corinthians 10:4-5

You also need to know God so intimately, you can be sure you're telling others the truth about Him. If you don't know it, you can't tell it. If you don't have it in you, if you haven't experienced His grace and truth, you can't share that from a place of vulnerability and authenticity with other people.

It's important that you share your experience of His truth with them and that you send them back to the truth to experience it for themselves.

Which is why I chose to put so much Scripture in this book and why I tell my clients and students often, *"Please don't just take my word for this. Don't go say "Katie said..." Go to the Word for yourself. Study what I'm telling you. Dive into God's Word. Let his Holy Spirit lead you into all truth."* His Words are the living, life changing, world changing words.

Howbeit when he, the Spirit of truth, is come, he will guide you into all truth: for he shall not speak of himself; but whatsoever he shall hear, that shall he speak: and he will shew you things to come. John 16:13

For the word of God is living and active, sharper than any two-edged sword, piercing to the division of soul and of spirit, of joints and of marrow, and discerning the thoughts and intentions of the heart. Hebrews 4:12 ESV

You need to know God in such a deep and familiar way because He has all the answers to life. He's given you everything you need for life and godliness.

According as his divine power hath given unto us all things that pertain unto life and godliness, through the knowledge of him that hath called us to glory and virtue. 2 Peter 1:3

My son, if thou wilt receive my words, and hide my commandments with thee; So that thou incline thine ear unto wisdom, and apply thine heart to understanding; Yea, if thou criest after knowledge, and liftest up thy voice for understanding; If thou seekest her as silver, and searchest for her as for hid treasures; Then shalt thou understand the fear of the Lord, and find the knowledge of God. Proverbs 2:1-5

If you seek it, you will find it, and what do you find when you find the knowledge of God?

Grace and peace be multiplied unto you through the knowledge of God, and of Jesus our Lord. 2 Peter 1:2

When you have knowledge of God; when you acutely know who He is, it changes your beliefs, which changes your thoughts, which changes your words, which changes your actions, which changes your outcomes and results. It changes everything about what you do in your life and in your business. And the result of profoundly knowing God is that overarching through line of grace and peace.

I explained in chapter 17 that one definition of grace is unmerited favor... My husband started several years ago to ask the Lord for favor during our family prayer time. It was amazing what we began to see! Asking for favor makes you realize that God is the giver of all, it also makes you realize that He's willing to give if you ask. It makes you anticipate finding His favor, and makes you realize just how much you already have.

My husband kept asking the Lord not only for His blessing, not only for His guidance and His protection, but for His favor, for His unmerited favor, for His grace to do what we needed to do. And for favor in the sight of other people, because that's also how God blesses. Luke 2:52 talks about how as Jesus grew up He *"increased in wisdom and stature and in favor with God and man."*

Tap was persistent in asking God for His favor every day that year, and we saw God do some amazing things. But here is the biggest blessing of all: we realized we don't have to ask Him for His favor, because we already have it. We needed to ask Him to help us *see* the favor He was already giving.

Ask God to give you eyes to see His favor and to experience the grace and peace that He promises to multiply to you when you know Him. He desires to give you more (Leviticus 26:9).

This entire book has been based on the fact that when you truly know God, you will have uninhibited access to divine enablement, His divine, unmerited favor that is abundantly above anything you could ask, think dream or dare imagine, much less deserve. As a believer in the secular marketplace, this is your unique flamingo advantage.

When you know who God is, the favor, the enablement, the help, comes from God who says, *"I called you to this. I'm going to do it through you. I'm going to give you what you need to do this successfully."*

The peace that passes all understanding (Philippians 4:7), and the sound mind that it is in Christ (2 Timothy 1:7); all of that comes when you know your God, not when you're distracted, not when you're running here and there and don't even have time to think or hear His voice.

It comes by knowing Him, by sitting at His feet, by meditating on His Word and consciously reminding yourself every day and in every situation, to ask, *"What do I know about my God, The Owner?"* and then based on that, *"How does He want me to respond? What is the next right step in my business?"*

Embracing your position in that relationship gives you a unique advantage. Anything is possible when you walk in that joyous freedom, my friend, and that is what I hope you have found as you've gotten to know Him better within these pages.

I look forward to hearing what God is teaching you and how He has brought you to a new understanding of Himself and His plan for the business he's entrusted to you during this reading experience. I would love to hear your testimony of what God has done. If you'd like to share it with me, please email me at Flamingo@KatieHornor.com.

And finally, remember, you've been brought to the Kingdom for such a time as this. Live in awe of the truth that God delights in you, has uniquely gifted you, and appointed you to do a special work for Him in the Kingdom. Go out and share His business with boldness and confidence in the world because the message of His love is relevant to every person you meet and sharing it is how you will change the world!

For Reflection:

My biggest takeaway from this book is....

My favorite quote from this book is...

The person I'd love to share this book is ________________ because...

I am uniquely equipped to run this business because...

My definition of business success is...

The truth I need to believe and act on is...

My next action will be...

I will take this action on/by (date)...

Note from Katie:

I hope you've enjoyed this book. If you'd like to see and hear me teach this content, I want to invite you to subscribe to the free on demand video class at www.HandprintLegacy.com/flamingobookclass

Or join our free community for Christian entrepreneurs: The Flamingo Sanctuary at www.facebook.com/groups/flamingobiz

There are 3 ways you can help others find this resource:

1. Please share your response as an Amazon review or post on social media and use the hashtag #MyFlamingoAdvantage. I look forward to reading your comments!
2. Gift a copy of this book to a friend
3. Invite me to speak for your event, mastermind or ministry group

Invite Katie to speak at your next event by visiting
www.KatieHornor.com

Katie's Podcast: TheFlamingoAdvantage.com/podcast

Connect with Katie on Social Media:

YouTube: @KatieHornorFlamingoAdvantage
IG: @KatieHornor @christian_business_events
Facebook: www.facebook.com/katie.hornor
LinkedIn: @KatieHornor
T: @Katie_Hornor
P: @KatieHornor

Get in touch to learn about the following programs and events:

- **Christian Marketing Retreat** - live event: How to Effectively Market your Business as a Believer in the Marketplace www.FlamingoBizEvent.com
- **The Flamingo Advantage Framework™**: Bible-based principles and Frameworks for marketing and client experience for modern Christians in business www.TheFlamingoAdvantage.com
- **Flamboyance™ Group Coaching:** Grow Your Business by implementing sound frameworks into a scaleable business process that won't compromise your faith, family or non-negotiables www.TheFlamingoAdvantage.com

- **The Queens Mastermind™:** Create a Business that Provides the Lifestyle and room for Legacy Activities that Light You Up in our Women's Higher-Level Business Mastermind www.QueensMastermind.com

Find More of Katie's Books at

www.theflamingoadvantage.com/books

End Notes:

[1] www.LaCasaRosal.com

[2] https://www.forbes.com/sites/christiankreznar/2020/09/16/small-businesses-are-closing-at-a-rapid-pace-with-restaurants-and-retailers-on-the-west-coast-among-the-hardest-hit/?sh=f6f407150330

[3] https://www.forbes.com/sites/shelleykohan/2020/02/09/mobile-commerce-to-grow-68-by-2022-as-more-people-shop-on-their-phones/

[4] https://www.npr.org/2022/01/12/1072057249/new-business-applications-record-high-great-resignation-pandemic-entrepreneur

[5] www.ClasicamenteAmigas.com

[6] www.DoingBusinesswithGod.online

[7] www.FaithLikeFlaminogs.com

[8] *God Owns My Business* by Stanley tam (Horizon House Publishers, 1969)

[9] Wisdom Meets Passion by Dan Miller (Thomas Nelson, 2012) pg.16

[10] www.HandprintLegacy.com/flamingobookclass

[11] www.HandprintLegacy.com/flamingobookclass

[12] *Faith Like Flamingos* by Katie Hornor (Katie Hornor, 2020) www.FaithLikeFlamingos.com

[13] https://webstersdictionary1828.com/Dictionary/glory

[14] www.facebook.com/poweredbysage

[15] https://womenwhochangetheworld.libsyn.com episode #14

[16] www.KingdomDrivenEntrepreneur.com

[17] *Faith Like Flamingos* by Katie Hornor (Katie Hornor, 2020) www.FaithLikeFlamingos.com

[18] www.KathyBurrus.com

[19] *The Marketplace Christian* by Darren Shearer, High Bridge Books, 2015) pg. 34

[20] www.Humorus.Co
www.KarinaLynnArt.com

[21] www.MattTommeyMentoring.com
www.ForYourSuccessPodcast.com episode #108

[22] www.JourneyBackQuilts.com

[23] *The Greatest Salesman in the World* by Og Mandino (Bantam Books 1968) pg. 58

[24] www.AlyssaAvant.com

[25] www.JoyfulNotes.ca

[26] www.PrairieDustTrail.com

[27] Bible Based Business by Jeff Testerman, (Jeff Testerman, 2011) pg. 62

[28] Bible Based Business by Jeff Testerman, (Jeff Testerman, 2011) pg. 62

[29] www.DanielleTate.org

[30] C.S. Lewis, *God in the Dock*, (Eerdmans, 1970) pg. 91

[31] www.HandprintLegacy.com/flamingobookclass

[32] https://www.merriam-webster.com/dictionary/aggregate#h3

[33] *Switch on Your Brain* by Dr. Caroline Leaf (Baker Books, 2015) ch. 15

[34] *The Incredibles*, Pixar/Disney 2004

[35] www.HandprintLegacy.com/courses

[36] https://handprintlegacy.com/plf-review
www.ForYourSuccessPodcast.com episode #168

[37] www.48days.com/eaglepreneur/members

[38] www.LaCasaRosal.com

[39] www.InSpitOfMyselfBook.com

[40] *Deep Work* by Cal Newport (Grand Central Publishing, 2016)

[41] *The 12-week Year* by Brian Moran (Wiley, 2013)

[42] *The Flamingo Biz Quarterly Planner* by Katie Hornor (Katie Hornor, 2020)
FaithLikeFlamingos.com

[43] www.MasterTeacherAccelerator.com

[44] https://believersportal.com/list-365-fear-not-bible-verses/

[45] https://en.wikipedia.org/wiki/State_Fair_(1945_film)

[46] *What Do I Know About My God?* by Mardi Collier (BJU Press, 2006) pg. 8-9

[47] Ken Collier, www.Wilds.org

YOUR MESSAGE MATTERS
#HUMORUSCO

Made in the USA
Monee, IL
13 April 2023